ALSO BY SUKIE MILLER

After Death: Mapping the Journey

FINDING HOPE
WHEN A
CHILD DIES

What Other Cultures Can Teach Us

Sukie Miller, Ph.D.

with Doris Ober

Simon & Schuster

SIMON & SCHUSTER
Rockefeller Center
1230 Avenue of the Americas
New York, NY 10020

Simon & Schuster and colophon are registered trademarks
of Simon & Schuster Inc.

Designed by Jeanette Olender
Manufactured in the United States of America

1   3   5   7   9   10   8   6   4   2

Library of Congress Cataloging-in-Publication Data
Miller, Sukie.
Finding hope when a child dies : what other cultures
can teach us/Sukie Miller with Doris Ober.
p. cm.
Includes bibliographical references and index.
1. Children—Death—Religious aspects.
2. Children—Death—Religious aspects, Comparative Studies.
3. Consolation.   I Ober, Doris.   II. Title.
BL625.8.M55   1999
291.2'3—dc21   99-21668   CIP
ISBN 0-684-84663-2

ACKNOWLEDGMENTS

Jason Lefer died in the winter of 1980. He drowned when he was fifteen years old. He was the first child I knew who died, and his parents were and still are my closest friends. The honor and the pain of being present to his departure and his parents' grief and healing were the seeds of inspiration for this book. I thank the Lefers for including me on their journey.

I am especially grateful to Edmundo Barbosa. As he did for my first book, Edmundo acted as guide and soulmate when I ventured into exploring ideas about what happens after death. For this second book his wisdom has guided me again. I thank him for his sage advice, encouragement, and constant good humor and love.

I am very fortunate to have friends and colleagues who helped me refine the book in its early stages by reading the manuscript and sharing their own stories, their expertise, and their sound advice. Thank you John Levy, Maggie DeCarvalho, Lucy Lamkin, Linda Pace, Robert Blau, M.D., Natalie Garfield, Martha Goldner, Chuck Houghton, Iza Barbosa, Stuart Miller, Ph.D., Richard Kirschman, Charlotte Taylor, Sandra Wright, Carole Levine, Trish McCall Friedman, Marilyn Kriegel, Jacqueline Bornhausen, Judy Skutch Whitson, Deborah Coreyell, Jill Marshall, Kenneth Ring, Ph.D., Baby Garroux, Nina Gorbach, Michael Roizen, M.D., and Anne Arensberg. Rachel Naomi Remen, M.D., gave generously of spirit, good advice, and cherished friendship. A special thanks.

ACKNOWLEDGMENTS

The following supported the research that provided the foundation for this book, and I am extremely grateful. My thanks go to The Life Bridge Foundation, The Fetzer Institute, Stephanie Stebich, Jeremy Waletsky, Charlotte Taylor, and my most inspired and inspiring friend, Marion Weber.

As with the last book, the indefatigable Barbara Lowenstein served me and the manuscript well as agent and friend. Laurie Chittenden's enthusiasm and editorial assistance were extraordinarily helpful, and Donna Gould's belief in "difficult" material and her unfailing work on my behalf (to say nothing of the Beanie Baby gifts) were above and beyond.

Also, thanks to Simcha Rafael for answers to all things Jewish, Don Flint (Vivacon) for library and Web searches, and Marty Moscoff for his last-minute save.

I am forever grateful to Joanna Slavin, assistant of thirty years, who with Harry, as always, held the fort.

And again, a round of applause to The Ink Blots. (You know who you are!)

Doris Ober and I collaborated to produce *Finding Hope When a Child Dies.* At times it was a very painful book to write. Your good humor, sharp mind, and inordinate skill made our work together rich, meaningful, and even—in the face of it all—fun. Thank you, my friend.

CONTENTS

CONTENTS

PART THREE

Questions When a Child Dies

The loss of our children affects us for as long as those children might have lived. We recall them at every empty milestone in the future—her senior prom, his graduation from high school—and years later, as the children of our friends live their rites of passage, we think, "It might have been my daughter marrying today" or "My son will never have children of his own."

It is this last aspect of grieving for a child that touched me most when I worked with bereaved parents, other family members, and even close friends who were long past their first raw grief over the death but were still brokenhearted years, sometimes even decades, later. To all the world they seemed recovered from their tragedies; they had resumed normal life. But in our private therapeutic hours together, I saw that this was not so: they did not feel "healed," and life was by no means "normal." Together we marveled at how present their lost children still were, at how profound the regret still was, at how their losses still shaped every single day.

I began to notice one thing these families had in common, no matter what the circumstance of their children's death, and that was a litany of very painful questions. They were questions I also found expressed throughout the literature of child loss, foremost among them being "Why did my child die?" "Am I somehow to blame?" "Will I ever see him again?" and "Can he hear me?"

We have no answers for these questions. We may eventually stop asking, but the case is never closed, the terrible wound remains open for a very long time, and the questions never go away.

In the 1980s I began to take time away from my regular practice for periods of travel and investigation into other cultural and religious belief systems, especially regarding life after death. At the same time I established a foundation called the Institute for the Study of the Afterdeath, whose purpose was to research other-cultural rituals, beliefs, and practices that relate to the afterlife.

To accomplish this, I organized a network of senior researchers in Africa, Indonesia, South America, and India. Most of these distinguished individuals were born into the cultures they studied, and all were well known to the tribes or religious groups I was interested in. They continued to work long after I left their countries, conducting interviews and filling out my detailed questionnaire with shamans and tribal elders in various parts of the world. *After Death: How People Around the World Map the Journey After Life* (Simon and Schuster, 1997) was the end result, a chronicle of how people across the world understand what happens to us after death.

I didn't focus on children in particular in my information gathering for that book. I assumed that the experience for children after death was the same as for adults. I wrote about where we go after death, not *why*. I didn't address those questions that haunt the families and friends of a child who has died, and when parents began asking me those same questions again at bookstores where I was invited to read, I seriously began to consider making it the subject of my next book.

I returned to my network of researchers and this time provided them with a questionnaire designed to explore the child's after-death journey specifically. I hoped in this way to find answers to some of those haunting and heretofore unanswerable questions.

Slowly fat manila envelopes began filling my mailbox, reams of pages full of detailed explanations and astonishing descriptions of what happens to Yakurr children and Indian children and Indonesian children after death. I went back to Brazil in the fall of 1997 and the spring of '98 to speak to Spiritists and members of the Umbanda religion, and to initiates of Candomblé about their children's journey after death. Among my friends and colleagues, many had also traveled extensively, and I discovered that they had many stories that were pertinent to this work. And so this second book began.

As I did with the first book, I collected these "samples" of various after-death beliefs and experiences in the classical way some scientists collect specimens. But the stories you'll read here from faraway places and the ones I'll share from my own practice and experience aren't meant to be scientific proof of any one particular theory or worldly wisdom.

For the most part, they are simply other-cultural realities that I believe can open doors for us and can sometimes open hearts—the open heart being one of the requisites for healing. I offer these examples and anecdotes as a way to begin speaking about a subject that is not easily spoken of in our culture. I offer them as a way to learn how other people answer those unrelenting questions for which we have no satisfactory answers.

In my first book I discovered among the fables, anecdotes, completed questionnaires, and "evidence" provided by shamans, priests, and other holy people a journey of four stages that adults travel to and through after death, and I structured the book according to these four stages: Waiting, Judgment, Possibilities, and Return. To my surprise, I found no such pattern to children's passage. The multicultural stories and experiences that I have collected about children, although equally rich, are diffuse and frequently contradictory.

But what I found most interesting in this second study was that

"Why did my child die?" and "Why has this happened to us?" are questions that *all* people ask, no matter what their ethnic or cultural background. *And elsewhere these questions have specific and concrete answers.* In many places the family of a child who dies, and the child's friends, not only know why he died and where he is but can check up on how he's doing, ritually offer him gifts and blessings, and continue to play a role in his life after death.

Imagine how it might be for us if we could follow our children's progress in some other world. Would it change how we miss them? Would it affect how we grieve? Would it help us heal? I think it would; I invite you to decide.

Together let us approach these universal questions about our children who have died, not as scientists but as *seekers*. We are seeking a language big enough to deal with the enormity of child death. We are seeking meaning in what seems senseless. We are trying to become whole people again, even if we cannot ever be the same.

This book is designed in three parts. Part One examines what our own cultural system teaches us about the death of our children. We look at how our limited language inhibits and obscures any satisfactory answers to the questions we have after our children die. And we look at the consequences that befall us because we can't adequately speak about or fully comprehend the death of a child we love.

In Part Two, I share the answers I learned on this most recent journey of exploration and discovery: how the Yoruba recognize a baby who is "born to die"; how the Buddha figure in Japan accompanies the souls of the dead newborn, and even unborn, into heaven; how the Hindus of India and Bali ensure admission and protection for their children in the afterworld; and many, many other beautiful, sometimes shocking, but all eye-opening stories.

In Part Three we move our focus from questions and answers and after-death systems to the shift that occurs in our own universe after the death of a child, and how this is common among all people but is experienced differently in other cultures. It is here that I think we can achieve some transcendence in our experience when a child has died—not only those of us who are parents and grandparents and siblings and extended family who have lost a child, but also those of us who don't know how to *be* with such stricken families.

The case histories you will read in these pages are from my own practice and that of other therapists who have been kind enough to share their professional experiences with me, or they are the personal stories of close friends. All the stories described here are true, but details have been altered in order to protect privacy, and some composite characters have been developed from several similar experiences.

In order to avoid frequent interruptions in the text, excerpts from the senior researchers' reports are not footnoted. Instead, the researchers are cited by name and affiliation with their particular groups in Appendix B, and all references to a specific group are attributable to that group's researcher. Some excerpts from the senior researchers' reports have been rewritten as dialogue to enliven the text.

On a personal note: I have never had children. I don't believe I could have written this book if I had. I think it would have been too personal, too painful, and that I might have been afraid to look too deeply or venture too far. But in writing this book, I refer to "all of us" who have lost children, and I do so to demonstrate how this most profound loss affects us all.

Finally, this book is written with great tenderness, especially for those clients and friends from years past and present who have made me aware of how complex a subject this is, and with an awareness that nothing I write will make it all okay. But in glimpsing the other ways people live with, think about, and accept the death of their children, I hope to make it easier for all of us to feel a little less fearful about what happens to the children we love when they die.

Opening our eyes to other people's realities opens our minds and hearts as well. In some of these realities we may find a word, an image, an idea, a key, a combination that can finally release us from wherever we have landed after the loss of a child. In some of them we may find one that satisfies the haunting question, "Why did my child die?"

PART ONE

CHAPTER ONE

We Have No Language

When your husband dies, you become a widow. When your wife dies, a widower. Children who lose their parents are called orphans. But we have no name for the parent who loses a child, nor for the brothers and sisters of a child who dies, nor for the others—aunts, uncles, cousins, grandparents, even the friends, contemporaries, and adults—who experience the loss of a child they love.

I hadn't realized the significance of there being no word for a child's survivors, and no word for the state of having lost a child, until I sat with those survivors over many years and began hearing the unpronounced fears that most people harbor for the children they love—for these almost seem built in, whether we speak of them or not.

The fact that there is no name for the one who has lost a child is of enormous consequence: the nameless live in a kind of limbo. They still exist, but in a new stratosphere where their namelessness effectively isolates them from the rest of the world.

When we don't name things, they remain out of reach. I have never known a parent or anyone else who has lost a child not to describe a period of feeling completely out of touch, beyond the reach of anyone else's comfort or understanding. And it's true. You can't engage on any deep level with someone whose name you don't know. You can't effectively ask for something that you can't name: "Bring me that—no that—no *that*!" is unbearably inefficient.

More than 145,000 infants, children, teenagers, and young adults die every year in this country alone. At least as many families experience a miscarriage or stillbirth every year.[1] So many people sharing a similar agony, and we have only the most halting language—a few poor adjectives for what our culture considers the most tragic of personal experiences. They say we are bereaved, or that we are distraught or inconsolable. But this hardly approaches our emotional state and doesn't nearly describe who we have suddenly become when our child or brother or sister or friend dies. Because we are no longer who we were, and we never will be again.

Language Is How We Relate

Language is how we relate to one another and the world. However it is expressed—spoken, or written, or sung; nonverbal, symbolic, even digital—language is what allows us to express what we feel, who we are, what we know. It is that crucial link between what we're experiencing inside—in the case of the death of a child, a unique combination of flashing turmoil that turns into grief that shifts to rage that becomes numbing despair—and what's going on around us: other people's shock, other people's discomfort, other people's efforts to help, and the whole wide world that incredibly, astonishingly, continues to rotate on its axis and go on, business as usual, as if nothing out of the ordinary has happened at all.

Without language it is difficult to *think*, let alone empathize. And when we are dealing with the unthinkable to begin with and then have no words with which to approach it, no wonder that psychological wisdom says that the death of a child is the most difficult death for survivors to endure. No wonder recovery seems so impossible.

Without language those of us who want to help our grieving friends or family members or devastated clients are groping in the dark. We may have the best intentions, but what can we say? And what can they say to us? So many people want to help, need to be helped, and yet we remain isolated from each other because there is no language with which to connect.

This is the way it is when we have lost a child. Not only are we without the words to adequately express what we are feeling, but those others who love us don't know what to say to comfort us.

Those things about which we cannot speak or will not speak do not simply disappear because we don't discuss them. In fact, they gain some of their power over us *because* we don't have language to vent them. They remain crouching in the shadows of our lives, unpredictable, a locus of rage, of despair, of fear, looking for an opportunity to be heard.

You don't have to lose a child to know what I'm talking about. Everyone who has ever loved a child fears the death of that child. I have known mothers to hold a mirror under a sleeping child's nose to assure themselves he is still breathing, and we have all met new parents who, overwhelmed by their infant's fragility, were afraid to pick up their baby because they might hurt her or drop her or accidentally cause her death. Some parents are so frightened by the possibilities that the big world may hold for their children that they severely compromise the children's independence.

Those fears beset us when we are deciding the rules by which our daughters may stay out at night; those are the fears about the stranger in the playground. That's us, silently thinking the unthinkable.

A symptom of how unspeakable this subject is is reflected in the way we respond to the deaths of other people's children. We cannot talk about the possibility of our own children dying—we can hardly bear to form such thoughts—because it seems too much like tempting fate. But a child's death that is a step removed is mesmerizing. We follow the stories of children who die with a real need to understand what happened and *why* such a thing could happen. We're glued to our televisions when such tragedies make the news, and then we want to read about them in the next morning's paper. It is not morbid curiosity that drives us; it is a *need to know,* and everyone who has ever loved a child has it.

And it has always been this way. Just reciting the names of our dead children—the Lindbergh baby, Adam Walsh, Megan Kanka, Polly Klaas, JonBenet Ramsey, Ennis Cosby—evokes extreme emotions.

But we need words and sentences, as well as concepts, for when our children die. Without them we cannot console or be consoled. Without them healing is a forever affair.

Beginning to Speak About
Death and Dying

In 1968, if we spoke about dying at all, it was in euphemisms. "She's not doing well" was about as explicit as we could be. We might bring ourselves to ask our doctor, "How much longer?" Everything was implied. And when people died, they "left us" or they "passed on." Because we were afraid or superstitious or embarrassed, we didn't speak about these things, and so we remained afraid, superstitious, and embarrassed about them.

This began to change in 1969 with the publication of an extraordinary book called *On Death and Dying* by Elisabeth Kübler-Ross. She became our first teacher in the language of life's last experience. And with the language we could finally begin to listen, begin to learn, begin to speak about such things.

Previously we thought about life and death as an on/off kind of thing. One was either active or inert, alive or dead. Dying meant simply that period just before death. We didn't often speak of anyone having a "good death"; we didn't distinguish ways of dying. We couldn't. We didn't have the language.

But Kubler-Ross told us that there are "stages" in the process of dying, and she named them: denial, anger, bargaining, depression, and acceptance. This sudden expansion of our language around a previously taboo subject flooded us with understanding.

By identifying and defining five specific stages in the dying process, Kubler-Ross provided us a vocabulary with which to begin to address, dissect, comfort, encourage, relate, empathize, and understand what was happening at the end of life.

Language, as I am using the word, is more than just a roster of words. It is also concepts and attendant practices. For example, at least once a year a banner is raised across the main street in the small town where I live that proclaims that it is Hospice Week. My town has an excellent hospital, and there is another fine hospital in a nearby town just thirty miles away. But we also have a hospice, a separate, acknowledged facility where we can go for help at the end of our lives, or from where medical and general care, counseling, housekeeping, and shopping help can be disbursed to our homes so that we may die in relative comfort, without great pain, still connected by virtue of proximity to those we love and who love us. During these caregiving-awareness days, many of the town's citizens and merchants have special fundraisers and sales to contribute in various ways to support our local hospice. This event is part of the new language developing around death and dying.

Before 1969 American communities had no social/medical structures dedicated specifically to the end of life. Today there are almost 3,000 hospices throughout the United States. Hospice, and everything it stands for, is both a result of and part of our new language and part of the ever-broadening discussion we have today on the subject of death and dying.

Since 1969 we have been adding to the language that Kubler-Ross began. Now we speak about near-death experiences, after-death experiences, and living wills. We discuss the "right to die" and debate the morality of "physician-assisted death." Today our "language" encompasses the psychology, the ethics, and the legalities that are part of dying. Today we can discuss openly what would have been considered "gory details" yesterday and avoided. We can talk about what we are dying of and precisely how we are dying of it. We can also talk about our grief around the subject of death as we never could before, expanding even more the language with which to address it.

Language is in every way an antidote to our fears and anxieties and general paralysis on the subject of death and dying. Language allows us to describe what happens, what is going through our minds, what we feel and have felt. Language lets us give sequence to events, render details and identifying marks. In all these ways we form definitions, and by doing so, we establish a common ground from which to speak.

With language what was amorphous takes shape. Whatever the subject, language brings it to life, and this is true even when the subject is death.

Once we find the common ground of language, we can develop treatment plans, erect facilities for the comfort of the dying, ratify laws that assist the dying, argue ethical standards regarding the treatment of the dying, seek comfort for the one who is dying, take comfort from others, and begin to heal. Without language we can do none of these.

With language not only can we name what we couldn't name before, but we may also be able to see what we couldn't see before. With language whole worlds open up to us. In some places that access may extend to the world where our deceased children reside.

Beginning to Speak About the
Death of Children

When my first book was published, I was asked to do readings at bookstores and on radio shows across the country. The readings were intimate: thirty or forty people would come to meet me, listen to an excerpt from the book, and ask questions. I loved meeting my readers. The radio shows were the opposite of intimate, though I liked them too: they were wide open, disembodied. But as different as the radio stations were one from the other—from Christian stations to liberal ones—and as different as the bookstores were—big chains or small independents—what never varied was the call or question about a child who had died.

After the readings, when someone approached me or courageously raised a hand or called in to the radio station to ask specifically about a child who had died, I noticed that they almost always whispered.

"My baby died two months ago," one woman said softly at Readers' Books Store in Sonoma, California, and everyone in the room leaned forward in their seats to hear her better. "And I just wonder if there's something I could be doing for him *now*."

"My younger brother was killed in a drive-by [shooting]," one late-night radio caller in New York City reported. "I felt him with me all the time for three months after he died. I think he even talked to me. 'Hang in there,' you know. But now he doesn't talk to me. Have you ever heard of that?"

"Do you think I'll ever see my daughter again?" a father inquired by phone on an afternoon radio show in Texas on which I was a guest.

There was so much *unsaid* in those plaintive comments and questions, whether they were delivered in person or over the air. The grieving mother at Reader's Books could not expand on what she had asked about helping her child now. She feared looking foolish. She believed that no one could understand. Was she really asking if there is life after death? Did *she* even know what she meant?

The Language Exists in Other Cultures

There are many places all over the world where that mother not only would be understood but would receive a detailed answer to her question, "Can I help my child now?" In some cultures she would be assisted in asking her child directly what he needed. In other cultures her spiritual counselor, shaman, or priest could divine her child's needs and assist her in meeting them.

I have been to a shop in Singapore where cartons of utilitarian items for the dead were stacked floor to ceiling. In parts of India, elaborate rituals after the death of a child ensure the child's acceptance in the next life and a better life thereafter. In places in Africa where the afterworld is fraught with danger, parents make offerings to gods who will see to the safety of their children after death.

In many African, Indian, Asian, and Indonesian societies, to name just a sampling, a history of intimacy with child death provides a language with which to talk about it, understand it, and make provisions for it. In such places where the language exists, the man whose brother "talked" to him after death would discover how common a phenomenon this is, and the father who wondered about seeing his daughter again would be reassured by countless others—perhaps the majority of people in the world.

In places where *language* encompasses concepts and beliefs, feelings and awareness, rituals, prayers, and other spiritual practices—in addition to the narrower meaning of a lexicon of words—thinking about, speaking about, understanding, and providing for such tragedies is how families and friends recover from them. It is not the same in our culture. What gets in our way? Why, when we have made fair progress concerning our deaths as adults, do we continue to whisper about the deaths of our children?

In the next chapters we'll take a look at some of the traditions and experiences that contribute to our limited language on this subject and our limited success in recovering from the loss of a child we love.

CHAPTER TWO

Our Mirror of God

Daniel and Evelyn's Story

It was not a large group that gathered to say good-bye to Jesse, one of twins not yet four years old. His parents, Daniel and Evelyn, performed their farewell ritual on a California hillside that had been scorched bare by fire the year before and now bristled with wildflowers, soft thick stands of pink and white lupine, spears of blue iris, buttercups, and poppies. Behind them many homes that had been lost in the same fire were at various stages of reconstruction, including their own. But there were other lots that were not being restored, that had not been touched, where only a blackened stone or brick fireplace remained standing in the rubble.

Twenty or so friends and members of the family stood in a rough circle. Several people held hands. Before the fire the hill had been clotted with scrub pine and coyote brush. Flowers had never grown there. "I take it as a sign that rebirth is possible," Daniel said, gesturing at the wildflowers that stood thigh high around them. "I'm trusting things will look beautiful again."

Almost everybody spoke in turn, clockwise around the circle. Many referred to the toddler as an angel. Daniel's own father thanked heaven for his remaining grandson, Frank, Jesse's twin, who was identical to Jesse in every way except for the anomaly, a defective heart valve. Jesse's nine-year-old sister spoke directly to him, "We'll take good care of Frankie for you, Jess." Evelyn could not say anything at all. Frankie held tight to her hand.

When it was Daniel's turn again, Evelyn handed him a ceramic bowl that held their child's ashes, and Daniel turned the bowl so that the wind could catch them as they spilled. The ashes were light, and the wind took them easily.

Winnie's Story

In an upper-middle-class suburb of Boston, the large church was filled to capacity. Family was there, of course, and friends of the family, neighbors and business associates, and friends of Jill and Seth, high school sweethearts, both in their late twenties, who had been married in the same church less than a month before. Although their wedding had been enormous, there were even more people at the high mass that marked their funeral.

The couple had been brutally murdered while on their honeymoon, apparently in a botched robbery. The sensational nature of the tragedy had attracted the media. Two television cameras and their operators, along with sound crew, were there. Jill and Seth had been a merger of two old Bostonian families—an exemplary couple, attractive, respectful, responsible, with everything going for them, bludgeoned to death by a stranger. It was so crazy, so tragic, that it was still front-page news a week later, and people stood in the back of the church who had not known the young couple but had been drawn there by what they had read about them or heard. Everyone grieved.

Sunlight streamed through the high stained-glass windows, filling the vast space below with shafts of colored light. When the organ played its last chord, sporadic sobbing punctuated the silence that settled over the room.

The immediate families of the young couple occupied the first two rows of the church. Between them there were eight brothers and four sisters and twice that many aunts and uncles, who took up an entire second row themselves with their numerous children. Both sets of parents and grandparents survived Jill and Seth as well.

The mass took over an hour. Nearing the end of the service, the priest recited the familiar words from the book of Matthew: " 'Let the children come to Me, and do not hinder them; for to such belongs the kingdom of heaven.' "

Then he commended the souls of the two young people to heaven, where they would reside in a state of grace and where their love for each other would be made eternal. "For God so loved the world," the priest reminded the mourners, "that He gave His only Son, that whoever believes in Him should not perish but have eternal life."

Myra and Robert's Story

For weeks ten-year-old Sara had been looking forward to a ski weekend with four school friends. It was her first independent outing. Her parents, Myra and Robert, had no fears and no intimations of disaster. The girls had a ride to the ski area and would be staying with the parents of one of them, whom Myra knew, and Sara was a competent beginning skier. But on the second day something went terribly wrong. The girls decided to try an intermediate slope that trailed along the edge of a cypress forest. They negotiated two successful runs and, confidence high, took off for a third. Sara was going too fast. She veered to avoid a skier in front of her, lost control, and smashed headfirst into a tree.

29

The following evening their rabbi came to Sara's home. Relatives and friends paying condolence calls removed themselves to the kitchen and dining room to give Myra and Robert privacy.

The rabbi sat in an overstuffed armchair facing the couple. He pulled his chair closer to them and leaned forward to take their hands. They sat that way in silence, the murmur of their family behind them, a deep sadness palpable in the house. After a while the rabbi said he would like to tell them a Hasidic tale about the second-century scholar Rabbi Meir and his wife, Bruria. This is the story that the rabbi told:

> Rabbi Meir and his wife had a baby son, the apple of their eyes, the heart of their hearts. On an ordinary day, when Bruria looked in on her napping baby, she found him dead in his crib.
>
> That evening when the rabbi returned from temple, his wife greeted him with this question: "My husband, if you were loaned a precious jewel, couldn't you keep it—would you have to return it?"
>
> Rabbi Meir's look was surprised and disapproving. "Why, of course, you must return it," he said sternly. "What kind of question is that?"
>
> Whereupon Bruria led the rabbi into his son's bedroom. And the rabbi saw that his son was dead, and his heart was broken, and he wept.[1]

A God-Centered Theory

Jesse's and Sara's parents and Seth's grandmother became my clients many years after their children's deaths, the stories of which I've tried to retell above as they were described to me. I was painfully aware of the limitations of our language as I listened to each of them struggle to tell me about the children they had lost, about their relationships to them, about the day of their deaths, about the funerals and memorial gatherings, about their feelings and fears and wild thoughts after all these years, about being "over it" yet still not over it, about not being able to break out of the strange twilight zone that their existence had been in since their children had died.

Looking for ways to make our time together easier, I explored the vast array of self-help literature written and frequently published by bereaved parents, hoping to find a language that would help us better communicate. In these books and pamphlets, parents share how they came to terms with their loss, offering themselves as examples that there can be life for the survivors after the death of a child.

These moving accounts helped a lot. They also helped me to see a recurring theme in the lessons they offered, one I heard echoed in therapy sessions, sometimes overtly stated, often not: regardless of whether we quote scripture or attend church regularly, no matter what religion we do or do not follow or grow up in, our overriding system for coping with and understanding the loss of a child is both biblical and God centered.

By this I mean that the death of a child is seen as God's will and the child is considered to have "returned" to God. It all comes back to God in the end. The "jewel" in the rabbi's story, symbol of the dead child, had to be returned to the "friend"/God who had loaned it. The priest at Seth and Jill's funeral had said the same, that the young couple was going back to God: "Let the children come to Me . . ." Even at Jesse's non-religious memorial, more than one person put the little boy with the angels.

Our strong orientation toward God, His responses, His grace, His punishments, His demands, His mysterious ways, and our ubiquitous belief that God has taken our children back when they die, have had an indelible influence on how we understand child loss. For many of us, that influence proceeds directly from the Bible in both the Old and New Testaments.

Fathers and Sons

Do you remember the story of Abraham and Isaac? In my Sunday school class we had a coloring book to accompany our lessons. Abraham, who is known as the father of the Jews, had a long beard and robe; his son Isaac, a boy about my own age at the time, stood alongside him in a short toga. Behind them lay a neat bundle of dried branches. I remember dutifully coloring while our teacher told us how God asked Abraham to make a sacrifice of Isaac.

> Some time later, God tested Abraham. And He said to him, "Abraham."
> And Abraham said, "Yes?"
> And God said, "Take your son, your darling, whom you love, Isaac, and go to the land of Moriah, and burn him there as a sacrifice on one of the hills that I will show you."[2]

And Abraham was going to do it! Would have done it, for sure, if God hadn't intervened. "Just a test!" God said. "Only joking!" Or at least that's what my startled eight-year-old sensibilities heard.

The story of Abraham and Isaac, known formally as the *Akedah,* or "The Binding of Isaac," has troubled scholars, psychologists, artists, clergy, and philosophers through the ages. Interpretations coexist from the sublime, like Rembrandt's exquisite painting *The Sacrifice of Isaac,* to the mundane and the scholarly, as in the anthologies of legends and lore and the analytic works connected with God's command to Abraham to offer Isaac as a sacrifice.[3]

In this pivotal tale of the Old Testament, we watch as a father walks up a hill with his son, intending to kill him. We listen for the father to protest. We wait to hear him say, "God, do not make me responsible for the death of my own child!" But amazingly, he does not protest. Abraham, who has challenged God on previous occasions, is as still as the hills of Moriah.

This same theme, of the parent *willing* to give the life of his own child, resonates perhaps even more profoundly throughout the New Testament in God the Father's sacrifice of His own Son, Jesus.

This sacrifice is a cornerstone of Christian religion. Jesus' birth, death, and resurrection give meaning and hope to Christians all over the world, and yet at its core is an act that defies understanding, the Father's giving up the life of His beloved child. Also notable in both stories is the child's acceptance: Jesus, bleeding from the cross, says to his Father, "Thy will be done." Isaac innocently allows his father to bind him and lay him upon a pyre, then watches without speaking as Abraham lifts his knife to perform the sacrifice that God has demanded.

Certainly the language—the use of the words *father* and *son*—creates a bond between us and the principal characters in the Bible stories. I think that when boys and girls hear for the first time the story of God's sacrificing His Son for our sins, they identify with the son, Jesus, just as I identified with Isaac when I was a child.

These very powerful stories to which we are exposed as impressionable children become etched in our memory. They influence how we relate to our own children in the future and how we relate to their deaths. This is true even if we don't remember the stories themselves, even if we don't take them as lessons about God, about our parents, or about ourselves but consider them at face value, as literal truths. This is true even if we think of them as pure fairy tales. This is the way it is in our culture.

Myra and Robert, Continued

Sara's parents came to see me together several years after her death. They had both been raised in Orthodox Jewish homes, and although they considered themselves Conservative Jews now, they had observed the cultural Jewish rituals for the death of their child. They had remained at home for seven days, sitting *shiva;* they had observed the Sheloshim, another three weeks of grieving; they had continued mourning Yud Bet Chodesh the full year. Through all their misery, they had exalted God in their prayers.

The rituals had helped to a certain degree, Myra thought. By the end of the first year, they believed that they were past the initial horror. Both resumed their lives and careers. But nothing seemed to penetrate the thick grief that still wrapped around them like fog.

Sara had been born late in their lives, when Myra was thirty-nine and Robert forty. She was their only child. The rabbi's story had hit home: they had, in fact, considered Sara a gift from God.

As time went on, both Myra and Robert became anxious and then desperate to make some sense of what had happened to them. They couldn't accept the idea that their daughter's death might make no sense, might be "totally without meaning," as Myra put it. And yet, though they silently considered all suggestions, including the rabbi's "jewel" metaphor, none of the meanings they tried to ascribe to the loss of their child worked for them. They rejected that Sara's death was some kind of test; they rejected that God had called her back; they rejected the idea of pure accident; they rejected karmic payback for previous sins, theirs or possibly Sara's, as some well-meaning friend had suggested. They rejected all these ideas loudly and angrily in the safety of my office. They were in an agony of rejection. But outside the therapist's office, they were silent on the subject. Silent and alone.

I couldn't understand why they resisted every possible source of solace or comfort so vehemently, and I asked them directly. Robert's answer shocked me with its power and its pain. "I wish I could believe that she was with God," he said. "But if I believed that, then I would despise God."

Winnie, Continued

Seth's family was Catholic and religious. Of his father's five brothers, two were priests. It was one of them who encouraged Seth's grandmother, Edwinna, to see me nearly five years after the big church fu-neral in Boston.

I was instructed to call her Winnie. She was in her early seventies, tall, fine boned, elegant. Vanessa Redgrave will look like Winnie in twenty years.

Winnie was not happy to find herself in my office, but she came be-cause her son had told her to, and she came with an agenda. She was perfectly clear: Seth had been very special to her—for many reasons, not important to this discussion, she assured me. She could certainly under-stand that Seth was also special to God. Of course, there was the matter of the awful circumstances of his and Jill's deaths. But after all these years she had succeeded in subduing her mental films, the terrible day-dreams she'd had of what the last minutes of their lives must have been like. She had also finally put to rest the excruciating lament, "It should have been me. I'm old, I've had a complete life, and they had everything still ahead of them."

However, there were still a few problems, she reported, all efficiency. One was that she couldn't get out of her mind that God had taken Seth back because she hadn't done a good enough job looking after him here on earth. And although she had asked God for help in understanding where they had failed and she had tried and continued to try, every day, to accept His will in this matter, she had not yet been successful. She still had a deep feeling of personal responsibility that she couldn't shake. She was counting on therapy to help her succeed where she had failed.

Having rested her case, she sat back and looked at me expectantly.

Questions for God

These brief sketches are true stories, and they are also emblematic sto-ries. They represent many other cases and other stories told after the death of a child in support groups and in therapists' offices and across kitchen tables. They reflect the power and the limits of our language around the death of our children, and they reflect our ambivalent feelings about God and His role in our loss.

Although there are many people who do find solace in their faith and in the Bible, there are many people who, like Robert and Myra, do not. Meant to be healing, the rabbi's suggestion that their child had returned to God did little, in the long run, to soften their grief. It only raised excruciating other questions.

"Why did He give her to us if He only meant to take her?" Robert asked. "If there's a lesson here, what *is* it? Why won't God reveal it?"

"Surely He could have intervened," Myra said to me. "Why didn't He?"

One of the cruelest aspects of child death in the Western world is that our system asks us to turn to God for comfort at the same time it makes us suspicious that God is responsible for our pain—because He took our child away from us or didn't prevent our child's dying.

When Sara's parents imagined her returning to God, their reference was to a vengeful God whose mercurial nature frightened them. The Old Testament God required terrible tests of His followers. And Myra and Robert could ask all they liked, God didn't have to explain. He didn't explain His demand of Abraham that he sacrifice his son. He didn't explain why He suddenly relented. Myra and Robert became more and more estranged from their temple community, from their rabbi, from their God.

Such weighty questions as "Why did this happen?" are not asked only by adults. In *The Spiritual Life of Children,* author Robert Coles describes a group of five ten-year-olds responding to the news that one of their schoolmates has incurable leukemia:

The girl who brought the news did so in tears, and when I met the group of five children . . . our shared sadness was obvious. It was then that I heard God questioned as I never had before by children

explicitly "religious" in their backgrounds, educations, stated beliefs. *"How* can God let such a thing happen?" "Why—why does
He permit this?" *"What,* tell me, what has she done to deserve
this?" "Where is He, where is God?" "When you see a girl like her
get sick like that, you want to scream and scream, because God
must not know—He couldn't know and just sit back and do nothing!"[4]

It is natural that we question God, but I believe that Winnie's question, "Am *I* somehow responsible?" may be the most universal and the
most dreadful question that we ask when our children die—though the
thought is so awful that we may not ask it aloud.

Whenever I hear the question of responsibility come up around the
death of a child, I think of Abraham, who never begged, "Dear God,
don't make me responsible for my child's death!"

The Mirroring of God

In our culture, as God is our Father, so are we gods to our children. And
if the death (and even the near-death) of the child is God's will, and God
and the parent are so intimately identified, it is really not so strange to
find ourselves struggling not only with the question of why and how
such a thing could have happened but with an even more horrendous
question: If He could kill His child, the psyche "reasons," and I am
made in His image, then could *I* somehow have been responsible for my
own child's death?

What we feel and experience after the loss of a child doesn't have to
make sense. Although we all believe ourselves to be basically rational
people, we are also highly emotional people. We may "know" that our
child succumbed to a heart valve defect or at the hand of a stranger or by
total accident, but we are plagued nevertheless by a need for bigger rea-

sons than these and by questions that have to do with us and our relationship to the child and to God.

I believe that one reason we don't heal more completely when a child dies has to do with our identification with God and the niggling thought that He *and* we are somehow to blame for the child's death. I call this identification the mirroring of God. I believe it occurs in virtually every modern family in which one or more members of the family assume a godlike relationship toward other members of the family—usually an adult or adults toward the children. Mirroring God is the phenomenon of us masquerading as beneficent gods to our children.

We all do this, whether or not we are actually parents, because all adults are Parents-with-a-capital-P to our culture's children. And our children accept this unwaveringly, as Jesus accepted His Father's power over him, as Isaac did. We are the supreme beings in our children's lives from the beginning, and while they are children, they think of us as gods and act toward us that way. It's little wonder that before very long, somewhere deep inside, we, too, begin to think of ourselves as gods. We look into the bright eyes of our children and see ourselves reflected as heroes. We like what we see.

We are, after all, their creators. We are the rulers of their universe. Collectively, we decide when they can vote, when they may drive—we lay down the rules by which they'll live. Our children's survival, their safety, and their well-being depend on us. We *want* them to think of us as gods for their own sake and safety. Not only do we not disabuse them of their notion of us, but, in fact, we lay their shining reflection over our human one. And then we fall for the masquerade ourselves.

And when they die, whether they are our biological children or a neighbor's or a television star's—and no matter how they die, whether by accident, from illness, by murder, or by suicide—the masquerade of being a compassionate, loving God is over. The mirror shatters. And with it, our self-image and often our faith, not only in God and in ourselves but in justice, in fairness, and in the premises on which we have been raised, the way we thought the world worked, the way our children saw us, the way we understood ourselves, even the connection that we had to God—everything is broken up, everything goes to pieces.

Daniel and Evelyn, Continued

As was the case with Winnie, I met Daniel and Evelyn about five years after their loss. Their daughter, Jennifer, was now fourteen years old, and Frankie, Jesse's twin brother, was nearly nine. Jesse had died almost exactly to the day a year after the couple had lost their home in a fire. On the day a year later when they held their memorial to Jesse, they told me they had both been terrified of some third disaster.

The family had weathered the fire, the loss of their home and all their possessions and treasured family keepsakes. But Jesse's death, coming at the end of a long, hard year, on the anniversary of their other great loss, depleted what energy they had managed so carefully to preserve and build.

Evelyn was devastated. At first her heart was broken for Jesse and then for Frankie, who missed his brother so much. Then as she watched her husband's inexpressible pain and her daughter's valiant effort to stay upbeat, to try to lift the family out of their unhappiness, she grieved for them. Her own sorrow was kept subordinate to her family's.

Hardest hit was Daniel. The fact that they "still had" Frankie was no consolation, as Daniel's father had said it should be. If anything, as Frank grew into a sturdy, studious little boy, it only seemed to make the loss of his twin more acute. They would have looked alike. Would Jesse have been so solemn? How would their lives have been different if Jesse had lived? To Daniel it seemed they all were diminished. The rebirth in which he had expressed faith at his son's memorial on a flowering hillside on a sunny day in California eluded him. He threw himself into the construction of their new home with an almost fanatical fervor. His obsession with that excluded everything else, including his family.

But when their house was finished, he was forced to face his loss again.

Daniel was a talented architect and builder. He was successful in his career and earned a more than comfortable income. He had made his own father proud, which was terribly important to him. He had been father-provider extraordinaire for Evelyn and their children. That was the man he thought he was; that was the man he showed to the world and that he and his family believed him to be.

But Jesse's death demonstrated Daniel's own limitations and what he took to be his inherent untrustworthiness. Deep down, he believed his family couldn't, *shouldn't* trust or respect him anymore. When his mirror of God broke into pieces, his entire picture of himself also shattered. After five years he had not forgiven himself for Jesse's death. I wondered if he ever would.

CHAPTER THREE

The Seventh Guilt

When our children die and our mirror of God shatters, many things happen all at once. We enter a different world. We have no bearings. The only thing we carry with us from the world before is a pervasive feeling of loss and a subliminal sense of having failed.

What we perceive as our failures weigh on us, along with a terrible burden of guilt. The loss alone, the gaping hole left in our life after a child dies, would be enough to suffer with, but on top of this, when we have physically lost a child, we suffer inordinately more and for a very, very long time from an extreme, even crippling feeling of self blame and shame. Many psychologists have written about this fallout of guilt after the death of a child, and I'd like to review briefly what we know about it.

Six Kinds of Guilt

Research and counseling psychologist Dr. Catherine M. Sanders, herself a bereaved parent, identifies six distinct kinds of guilt that are common among families who mourn children. They are the guilt of helplessness, of survivorship, of ambivalence, of perceived misdeeds, of shame, and of co-dependence.[1] I've seen shades of each in virtually every grieving parent I have counseled, and most often several are active at once.

Perhaps foremost is the gnawing self blame and *guilt at our helplessness* to prevent the child's death. It expresses itself in our playing the child's death like a movie, again and again. We fast-forward, we rerun, we freeze frame after frame, image after image. We become witnesses in the horror story that is the death of our child, whether we witnessed it or not. Winnie's "terrible daydreams" of her grandson's violent death took years to squelch. Like Winnie, we relive the worst moment of our lives over and over, when our beloved child died, as if we could revise the ending and save her.

The *guilt of survivorship* made Winnie say, "It should have been me. They had their whole life ahead of them." But survivorship guilt has another level even deeper than this profound regret. It is unnatural for the child to predecease the parent. When we outlive our children, the world has been turned on its head.

We do a grueling review of our level of attention and devotion to the deceased child. We suffer the *guilt of ambivalence* when we remember that we were occasionally annoyed, that there were days when we resented the child. We know in our hearts that although we loved our child, we did not love her one hundred percent, one hundred percent of the time.

The *guilt of perceived misdeeds* is our perception that God is punishing us for our evil ways. This comes up even among people who don't think they are believers. Deprivation has always seemed a form of punishment; to be deprived of our child is surely the worst kind. Besides, the loss feels so much like a punishment, it's hard not to look to our own sins and for who might be meting out retribution.

Parents who work, especially mothers who work, accuse themselves of not having been there for their child, of having failed that way. We look for where we have fallen down on our job as a parent, where we have been sloppy in our level of care. We know that when we lose something it's a result of our carelessness—our own parents taught us as much. A voice inside us remembers the shame attached to having lost a valuable possession and applies it and amplifies it in this circumstance.

We review not only the past for our failures but the present as well. We are *ashamed* of how we respond and react to just about everything. I had a client who was mortified that she and her husband had made love on the night they buried their six-year-old daughter. "What's wrong with us?" she cried. We disappoint ourselves and berate ourselves: "I'm not handling things well, not feeling the right things, not making the right choices, not saying what needs to be said." We monitor ourselves and pass the sternest judgments.

We carry a burden of guilt in relation to our own parents that is exacerbated by our children's death. I suspect that Daniel was experiencing this in regard to his father, whose respect he was forever unsure of. With the loss of our children, we have failed not only them but our own parents; we have not measured up to their example or their standard—if we ever did. *Co-dependent guilt* means failing as the parents of our children *and* as the children of our parents.

Guilt Is Not for Adults Only

Feelings of guilt run rampant when a child we love dies, and such feelings are not reserved for adults only. The brothers and sisters and best friends of children who die also feel helpless and to blame. They suffer both sides of survivorship guilt. On the one hand, they believe that *it should have been me.* They will constantly compare themselves to their dead brother or sister or friend, and they may very well conclude that they are far less deserving of life than the superior sibling or best friend who died. It seems as if some terrible cosmic mistake has occurred.

On the other hand—and equally affecting in this area of survivorship guilt for the brothers and sisters and contemporaries of the child who died—there is the terrifying thought that *it could just as easily have been me!* The idea is unnerving. The notion of a safe world is dashed, and children will cling to their parents as never before. They, too, have been sick in bed with a fever. They have also run recklessly from between parked cars. Any of Sara's friends could have lost control on the ski slope that day. It could as easily have been one of them.

Like us, children feel as if there is something they should have done or not done to prevent their sibling's or friend's death—they know the feeling of having failed in some way. Even Thumpy the bunny admits at the end of *Thumpy's Story of Love and Grief* (a bestselling book for children who have lost a sibling), "Sometimes we still wonder if we did something wrong to make [our sister, Bun] die."[2]

But unlike their parents, children rarely would willingly exchange places with their deceased brother or sister or closest friend. Maybe it should have been and could have been them who died, but deep down they're glad it wasn't. This in itself is a cause of guilt.

For many siblings left behind, the death of a brother or sister causes the foundations of safety to crumble. They see their parents' pain and they are shocked by it. Do you remember how frightening it was the first time you saw one of your parents cry? Among our children, we "supreme beings" have a reputation for courage and strength. Parents aren't supposed to cry. We're supposed to be able to handle everything.

Our tears reinforce the helplessness that a surviving child feels because she couldn't prevent her brother's death and because her own survival isn't enough—she's not strong or good or smart enough—to make up for their loss. This was very much the case for nine-year-old Jennifer, sister of the twins Jesse and Frank. She struggled with the thought "If it had been me who died and Jesse who lived, my mom and dad wouldn't be so sad." To ease her parents' grief became Jenny's purpose. She became the "perfect" child.

The world changes as profoundly for the sisters and brothers of the child who has died as it does for their parents.

Layers of Guilt

It is not uncommon to see all six expressions of guilt in layers, nearly smothering the grieving family of a child who has died. They come in waves, sometimes crashing down simultaneously, sometimes unpeeling in long, slow, consecutive curls.

But over time—frequently over a period of three to five years, if not longer—each of the six kinds of guilt we've talked about responds to individual therapy, group therapy, and self-help groups. There are many groups to help the families of children who have died, and they are of inestimable value. Such a group may be general, open to all people who grieve a lost child, or specialized to support the families and friends of children who have died from suicide, in a car accident, prenatally, by murder, from cancer, and so forth. (A list of such resources appears in Appendix A.)

Yet, no matter how much time goes by, guilt still gnaws at us. When Winnie came to see me nearly five years after Seth's death, she had used her indomitable strength of character and her equally strong Catholic faith to strong-arm most of her guilts into submission. At our meeting she had already come to terms with her helplessness, perhaps because she knew she was helpless before God. She had accepted her own survivorship, her ambivalence, her regrets. She had worked through the layers of guilt she had lived in association with what had happened to her grandson—and still there was a feeling of responsibility she couldn't touch.

"Tell me a little about that feeling," I said to her on our first meeting. "Can you pin it down? In what way could you have been responsible?"

"In a thousand ways!" she said, barely concealing her irritation at my not understanding. "We must have left something important out of his upbringing that might have served him, saved him in that moment." She hesitated but forged ahead.

"For instance, I recall he wanted to take some karate class when he was eight years old, but it meant driving him across town, and neither his mother nor I thought it was important enough to rearrange our schedules to fit in one more activity. Maybe if we had taken him to those lessons he would have been able to defend himself that night."

A Guilt to the Seventh Power

Winnie's idea that her stance on the karate lessons twenty years earlier might have contributed to Seth's death was too irrational to qualify as the guilt of ambivalence or the guilt of regret. I believe that Winnie was expressing a kind of *causal* guilt that is peculiar to us in the West, that stems from our Judeo-Christian tradition, and that is bound up in our mirroring of God.

I'm tempted to call this unnamed guilt—which does not appear in any of the psychological discussions of the experience of parents, friends, and siblings of a child who has died—a seventh category of guilt, but it is really more like a guilt to the seventh power.

It is the terrible suspicion that we ourselves have killed our child. It is the guilt of our perceived responsibility. It is the assumption that our masquerading as God has somehow come to this. This is the price of our mirroring God. The seventh guilt says, "Some way, somehow, I *am* responsible for the death of my own child."

This unspoken, unseen sense of responsibility for which we have no language remains untouched by time, compassion, friends, and support. It is free-floating inside us. Long after the survivors have been patched back together, this seventh guilt remains, undiminished and unpredictable, like a virus, sometimes quiet, sometimes raging, *there*.

The seventh guilt is the great common denominator shared by almost every person who has lost a loved child. It affects women who have miscarried, women who have aborted their pregnancies, and parents and families who have lost a child of any age. I think it is a constant overwhelming, undermining obstruction to recovering from the loss of our children.

The seventh guilt is not connected to our helplessness. It is not about our survivorship. It does not relate to ambivalence over our imperfect love for our child; nor does it relate to our personal sins or our reactions to our loss or our earlier lives, for that matter.

In retrospect, my very first clinical experience with a bereaved parent was a painful lesson in how profound and tenacious this seventh guilt is. Josephine was widowed at an early age and never remarried. She was a single mother when that was not as common as now. We met for many weeks in the 1960s, during which Josephine could only review the ways in which she had contributed to, failed to prevent, and at least figuratively caused her nineteen-year-old daughter's death, which had occurred seven years earlier.

But really, what an astonishing idea, I thought at the time. Josephine's reasoning defied logic: her daughter had died in a commercial plane crash. Wasn't it outrageous of her to think she was in any way responsible?

"I was so selfish, insisting she come home for the holidays," Josephine said to me, gripping the arms of the chair. "If only I hadn't suggested she take an earlier flight. If only I had discouraged her going to a school so far away. . . ." She was drenched in blame and shame and the knowledge of her personal failure.

Now I believe that Josephine's pain was a result of the seventh guilt. In relation to her daughter, Josephine had assumed the role of God. She had "decreed" that her daughter should take the doomed flight. She had "ordained" which school her daughter would attend. Josephine had had the power to prevent the death of her daughter simply by saying, "Don't come." And she hadn't. In her own mind Josephine had delivered her own daughter to her death.

When Winnie wondered if she was responsible for Seth's death because she didn't drive him to karate lessons when he was eight, she, too, was in the grip of the seventh guilt. Her identification with God in relationship to her grandson was little different from Josephine's in her relationship with her daughter. The big problem both women struggled with was the same, the feeling that, like God, they had caused their children's deaths.

Elizabeth Cohen writes movingly of losing her baby in utero in an essay entitled "The Ghost Baby" in *The New York Times Magazine:* "For a while I kept my miscarriage secret, which felt as if I were holding my breath. Then I went through a period when I told everyone I met. I could see some people blush, not sure how to react to this confession of pain. Some days still I feel like a murderer."[3]

Our mirroring of God is one of the pitfalls of believing that we are made in God's image. Many people are never disabused of their identification with the Supreme Being, but if you have lost a child, you become blindingly aware of how far you are from being God and how far you are from being in control of anything at all.

Winnie, Continued

Winnie, who had been reluctant to consult over her very private grief, did continue to do so, to our mutual surprise. Unlike Evelyn and Daniel's generation, Winnie hadn't grown up on self-help books. She was of the keep-your-problems-to-yourself school. We made a pact that we would meet four times, after which we would evaluate our progress and decide whether to continue. Four sessions later we agreed to try another four.

It was then that I broached my idea about the seventh guilt and how it is caused by our mirroring of God. As the matriarch of her family, Winnie occupied an exalted position. Her sons and daughters and their children were not unlike a devoted congregation. I believed Winnie's inability to shake her feeling of responsibility for Seth's death was based at least in part on her having mirrored God. I wondered if she could relate to the idea and if she would agree.

At first she was shocked at the suggestion that she might ever have "played" God. Winnie considered herself God's servant. But then she remembered a moment from her childhood when she was very young —five or so years old—lying in a meadow, watching a small ant army on the move, and thinking that to those ants she could easily be God. "It may have been the first time I'd ever seen things from another perspective," she said. "The idea was really quite thrilling."

And she had indeed felt something similar when her children were born, she said, combined with awe and joy at what she and her husband had created.

Yes, she had seen herself as all-powerful and all-responsible as a parent and a grandparent; she recognized that. In fact, she had loved the feeling. It was she who explained to the children where the sun went at night, she who banished the monsters from the closet, she who commanded the respectful obedience of all the members of the family.

After a long silence she said quietly, "If the truth be told, it's the feeling that all my power was taken away with Seth's death that makes life so empty now." And then she interrupted herself: "So it is God's punishment, after all. For having overstepped. For even thinking for a minute that I was Him. For having forgotten my place."

But mirroring God is not blasphemy. It is part of the human condition for all of us in the West. We are programmed for it, beginning when we ourselves are very young and look up to our own parents as gods.[4] It is reinforced when we learn the connection between God and

49

Father in our Bible stories. And it is locked into place when *we* become parents. It isn't a problem until our children die.

If only I had known then what I know now. Winnie was flexible enough to look at life from more than one perspective. I think she would have been moved by many of the other ways of thinking about the death of children that I have learned from other cultures in the years since we met in therapy sessions.

I would have liked to tell Winnie about a religion in which it is inconceivable that God would exact punishment with the life of a child. For instance, I could have talked to her about the followers of the Baha'i faith, who believe that life on earth is just an interlude on our soul's great journey, which includes rebirth into many worlds other than this one and ultimately an actual merging with God.

Baha'is understand that they are in this world in order to prepare for a complex next world. In the course of this life, they are collecting what they will require for the next, and in the next world they will be acquiring what will be necessary for the world after that, and so forth. For the Baha'is, the death of a child indicates that the child has achieved the necessary qualities for the next life "soon enough."

Or it may mean that to continue this life would be detrimental to preparation for the next. Our senior researcher in India tells the story of a Baha'i woman who inquired of the prophet Bahaullah why her son had died in childhood. She was advised to be patient and wait for the prophet's answer. Some time later she had a dream about her son as an adult. The dream showed her a future she would never have imagined—her son as an angry, violent man assaulting another man and taking his life. The dream was evidence for this grieving mother that an early death had saved her child from a crime that would have landed his soul in hell.

Not that I would want to convert Winnie to the Baha'i religion or any other way of thinking. But I have seen stories like these open the eyes and hearts and imaginations of people who have lost children they love. I have seen them provide a language, through shared experience, for beginning to understand that loss. And I have seen how opening—disclosing, uncovering, exposing, revealing, and then freeing and releasing—is how we can loosen the grip of the seventh guilt and get beyond just surviving the deaths of our children.

CHAPTER FOUR

Freezing in Time

Along with our lack of a broader vocabulary that could help us understand what has happened after a child's death that could help us heal, and along with the guilt that impedes our healing, is a third, distinctly Western phenomenon that frequently prolongs our agony. As with the mirroring of God, it is not something we talk about—not part of our language—but it is easily observed to some degree in nearly every family that grieves a lost child. I call this third problem *freezing*.

There's a distinction between freezing our children and keeping the memory of a loved child. The difference is the difference between rigidity and flexibility, and it affects the entire experience of our grief and our potential for healing.

We never want to forget our dead children, and there are many ways to keep their memories without turning them into eternal ice sculptures. We plant a tree to live on in the memory of a child, donate a bench in a park in her name, endow a scholarship, even make the gift of our dead child's organs—these are all ways we honor our children and preserve our memory of them.

We preserve them in more personal ways as well, with the photos on the mantel, the flute kept safely in its velvet-lined box, the trophies on the bookcase, the sweater beginning to wear at the elbows. We want and should have keepsakes. These things keep our sense of our child alive even after he is gone.

After Sara died, Myra and Robert gave each of the four girls who had been with her on her ski weekend a small framed photograph of her. These gifts became treasured mementos. But too many such remembrances can come between us and the child we loved. When the child's presence after death is as constant and considerable in a home as when he lived, freezing is very likely going on.

Freezing Through the Physical

The first and most common sign that we are freezing our child is when we begin to make a fetish out of those things that belonged to him, that he loved, that when we see them infuse us with the spirit of the child. This kind of freezing shows itself in homes where what looks like an altar, erected spontaneously in the days after the child's death, remains permanent long into the future, or where an *inordinate* number of photographs serve as permanent memorials on walls and tabletops and mantelpieces, or when a room appears as if the child still lives there.

My clients Barbara and John were a couple who had frozen their child in this way. Zach's room had been left unchanged since the day he walked out of it six years earlier to die in a car crash. The room was a space suspended in time. Posters of rock stars now years out of fashion still hung on the walls; the book *Moby Dick* still lay open face down on the desk. Zach's clothes still occupied the closet and drawers.

We had been meeting for a couple of months before I knew that Barbara had memorialized Zach in this way. It came up as a point of contention for the couple. John couldn't bear to go into Zach's room anymore, but it was a refuge for Barbara.

"In the beginning I sat on his bed and just cried," Barbara said. "But now it's a place I can be with him and speak to him, and it makes me feel good to do that. Sometimes I believe he answers me."

That kind of talk made John very uncomfortable. He wanted to "get over it, heal, whatever you call it," and he thought that Zach's room had become too important to Barbara. He believed it kept her grief too raw. And it was painful for him. It served to keep his sorrow alive when he was looking for ways to end it. He wondered whether Barbara really wanted to feel better, whether she had any interest in returning to any kind of life together.

He was angry and impatient and terribly, terribly sad. He had lost his son, and now his wife was slipping away. "You'd rather be in the company of ghosts than with me!" he accused her.

But it wasn't a matter of the company of ghosts for Barbara. Our children are typically the objects of our greatest interest and concern. When the child dies, we can't just *stop* caring. It's unbearably hard not to wonder where he is, what he's doing, how he feels—even though we think these are "crazy questions." And when we are unable to find answers to these crazy questions, we will very frequently freeze our children in a place where they used to be, in that time when they lived with us and we did know where they were and what they were doing and how they felt. If Barbara had known where Zach was and that he was comfortable and that he was all right, she would not have had to keep his room for him at home.

Barbara didn't need the room in order to "communicate" with Zach. She could do that anywhere. She used it as a haven because it was a place out of time where she could pretend that Zach wasn't dead, where everything remained as it was *before*. "When I'm in his room," she confessed to John in my office, "Zach is alive again."

Freezing a child in his previous time and space as Barbara did is a way of erasing everything from the moment of the child's death straight through to the present. Freezing is a way we desperately try to keep our children in this life, a way we passionately deny that they have left us.

Freezing Oneself in Time and Place

A client of mine in California was offered the deanship at a prestigious eastern college. His twenty-one-year-old daughter had died of leukemia seven years prior. "Before, my wife and I would have considered this move a heaven-sent opportunity," he said. "But when it came down to it, we couldn't leave the place where our daughter grew up. It probably sounds crazy. Maybe if we were younger parents—but we put half our lives into this child in this place. It's hard to walk away from that, from her. It feels like, if we walked away, we'd lose her a second time."

As poignant as this father's deep attachment to the place he associated with his daughter was his inability to "move on" with his own life after her death. This is another expression of how we can become "frozen," in this instance in time and place.

This family had the luxury of choosing to decline their job offer. But sometimes we have to move or make a change that forces us to set aside our "freeze frame" of the time before, and this can be a wrenching experience, calling up fresh grief even after a very long time.

It is common for people who have frozen a lost child to be more resistant to changes in general. Sometimes this resistance expresses itself very subtly. One of my very close friends continues to wear her hair as she did in the early 1970s, when her daughter died, even though she "hates" her hair this way and is always going to make an appointment to change it. A client of mine adopted a new clothing style completely when her son died—solids only, and only light colors—and hasn't deviated from that dress code in fifteen years.

Freezing Feeling

Sometimes people suffer a kind of inner freezing, different from emotional coldness or the numbness many people feel after a tragedy. Emotional numbness is temporary. Emotional freezing is not; it effectively halts one's feeling life around the loss of the child. My client Regina is a good example.

Her older son, Peter, died of lymphoma at the age of thirty, when her younger son, Mickey, was nineteen. As a gesture of their solidarity, six of Mickey's college friends drove ten hours from school to attend the reception after Peter's funeral. They arrived at Regina's home when it was overflowing with Peter's friends and relatives, his wife's family and her colleagues, his business associates, neighbors, community leaders. There were literally hundreds of people in attendance late into the day following the early-morning funeral.

After Mickey's friends paid their respects, they took Mickey off to a coffee shop. He was gone for no more than an hour. But Regina was furious. She considered it the height of insensitivity that Mickey had left the family on the day of his brother's funeral to be with his friends. And she never really got over it.

Two years passed. Mickey graduated, married, and had a child of his own. Today he is a successful teacher at a prestigious community college and is known to be a helpful, kind young man. He's a Big Brother to two inner city kids, active in his church and in his community.

Mickey is someone who will be there for you, and everyone who knows him knows this, except for one person. His mother.

When Regina speaks of her second son, it's as someone not to be counted on, as someone who will disappear when you need him—which is so far from the truth about Mickey as to be absurd. Regina has frozen her feelings at the time of the death of her first son, and those feelings have become her point of reference.

Although she learned that parents and siblings grieve differently, what she saw as Mickey's irresponsibility toward his family at Peter's funeral has gotten stuck, and Mickey's and Regina's relationship with it. Anything that happened before or after doesn't count.

This kind of freezing locks us out of life and in with death, with ghosts, and with fantasy. This kind of freezing won't let us be with the rest of our family, who live on the other side of the door that's frozen shut and who may need to know that we are still there for them as well.

Freezing in Time vs. Actual Time

A woman came to see me about her problems around the subject of aging. It was several sessions later that I discovered she had lost a son years before. When we began to explore the connections between the loss of her child and the loss of her own youth, she said quite thoughtfully, "You know, it's not exactly that. It's that I grow away from him as I age."

Her child had stopped aging at the moment of his death, but she could not. Instead of time healing her wounds, time was pushing a wedge between her son and herself, and every wrinkle, every physical limitation declared to her that she was moving away from him—fresh cause for pain after all these years.

A child dies. Time passes. Ten years, fifteen, twenty years pass and we are very changed from that time when the child lived. We don't look the same as when our child knew us; we can't do the same things. We aren't even the same people. Our backs ache. Our knees are stiff. Shooting hoops with a preteenage son would be just about impossible today. Today we might not even *want* to spend all day Saturday shopping and baking for a child's birthday party, blowing up a hundred balloons, cleaning up afterward.

All of what we used to do and can do no longer reminds us of the widening gap between us and the child we have frozen in time. Parents who have lost children have another layer to deal with in the aging process: every gray hair takes us an increment further from the child we are desperate to hold close.

Ten years after Sara's death, her mother, Myra, called me. She and

Robert had ended therapy with me several years earlier. Now Myra was about to turn fifty, and many issues had come up for her, including issues she thought she had resolved about Sara. We made an appointment to meet.

She had changed. She was not the woman in agony that I had known before, though there was an intensity about her still. Her dark hair was now streaked with gray; she wore a light lipstick and no other makeup.

"The other day it occurred to me that Sara would be twenty years old now," Myra said. "I never think of her as anything but ten, but I was looking at myself in the mirror, and I imagined I saw her at twenty. We had the same eyes. . . ."

She said she felt as if she were losing Sara again, as if Sara were another part of her youth that was fading incredibly fast right before her eyes. "I didn't think aging was going to be a big deal for me," she said with a wry smile. "But it is, and part of it is this ridiculous idea that soon Sara won't even recognize me."

Myra's experience in front of the mirror had allowed her to see through the image of the ten-year-old girl frozen in her memory. For just a moment Myra had glimpsed a world in which a child continues to exist and to age after departing this life.

Frozen time doesn't move; actual time does. As we age, actual time goes by faster and faster, ever accelerating. If we have frozen a child in our past, we may feel as if we're standing on the back of a fast-moving train, waving good-bye to her.

How Freezing Affects the
Surviving Children

Parents should be especially attentive to their surviving younger children when they reach the age at which their older brother or sister died. Many children have the deeply held idea that they will not, maybe *should* not, outlive their sibling. When they do, they may feel terrified that they are moving into some dangerous, uncharted territory. Until now the older brother had paved the way; until now they could follow his example. Survivorship guilt may revisit now—even many years after the fact. It can be a time of great inner turmoil that coincides with a major revision in family structure. This was how it was for Sammy.

Sammy was a middle child, nine years old when his brother, Rodney, committed suicide at the age of sixteen. Their sister, Leah, was five. When Sammy turned fifteen, "something radical happened," his mother told me. Once eager for school and known as a good student, now Sammy was frequently late, and his grades dropped precipitously.

He instructed everyone at home and at school to call him Sam from now on, and although this lightened his mood for a while, it didn't last long. He became lethargic and sullen once again, and his grades continued to slide.

It may sound like Sam was going through normal teenage angst, even without the loss of a sibling, but there was definitely another problem present. Soon he would turn sixteen, and many things would change for him, not only his advancement deeper into adolescence. At once he would become older than his deceased older brother. Suddenly he would no longer be a middle child. Suddenly he would become Leah's *only* older brother.

As long as Rodney stayed frozen in place at the age of sixteen, all went well with Sam. But approaching the same age as when Rodney died, Sam had to deal not only with normal teenage confusion but also his changing identity and position in the family.

A colleague of mine worked with another youngster in a very similar circumstance to Sam's. This was a case of two sisters, one of whom died of a drug overdose at the age of eighteen. When the surviving sister turned eighteen, she flunked her senior year in high school, ensuring that she would be kept back and not have to venture beyond where her sister had gone in school. It was the younger sister's way of trying to freeze *herself* in that time when her sister lived.

I've noticed that brothers and sisters who lose a *younger* sibling, and their parents, are less likely to engage in freezing than the survivors of an *older* child. But in families where the effort to preserve the deceased younger child does occur, an older sibling may have to deal with feelings of personal rejection, of profound sadness, or of anger at not being able to compensate for the child who died.

Moving beyond the age at which a sibling or even a young friend died can also be a time of great release, or "unfreezing," for the surviving child. But even this comes with built-in guilt. Eighteen-year-old Bert died when Harold was eleven. Seven years later, when Harold had outlived his brother, he broke an invisible barrier. Harold had always compared himself to Bert and suffered in comparison. Now he slowly began to let go of that inner competition that he always lost, but at the same time he suffered feelings of disloyalty toward his no-longer-older brother for having succeeded him.

We do not purposely freeze our children or brothers or sisters or childhood friends who have died, but the tendency to do so is part of our natural desire to keep them alive, and that is as natural as breathing. Sadly, though it seems to offer some comfort at first, freezing is more often a great disservice than a healing act to our families and ourselves. It does not soften the blow of having lost something so precious as a child. Ultimately, this extreme expression of keeping our children with us after death only keeps the sorrow alive, as Zach's father, John, said it did.

Of course, we still want our children with us, but being with us is no kind of life for them anymore. Although Zach may have been "present" in his preserved room, he didn't live there. He couldn't bring Barbara new pleasures; she had only the old ones to review and review. Barbara believed that Zach's room made her feel good, but in the long run it kept his absence constantly in the foreground of her consciousness, kept the wound open, kept her from her husband and him from her, and kept them both from the possibility of comforting each other.

In cultures in which it is understood that children continue to have a life on the other side of death and a future in worlds after life, their families think as much about what those children are doing *now* as they do about what used to be. If a parent tried to freeze a child in time after death, he would be considered to be interfering with the way life and death works and with the child's destiny in the future. Among those systems that believe in reincarnation, return, or resurrection, freezing in time would be disastrous to a child's future in subsequent lives. It just isn't done. More about this in Part Two.

PART TWO

Answers When a Child Dies

It's not that we *blame* God for the death of our children, exactly. It's more that we blame God for His refusal to answer our questions about their deaths, questions that haunt us from the moment the child dies and continue to do so through all our subsequent years. Because of this, in the course of our grieving, it is not uncommon for some people to feel resentment toward God or to reject Him or to take it as the ultimate evidence that He doesn't exist at all.

Then those most difficult questions that come to all bereaved families at some point boil to the surface, often long after the death of the child. Sometimes, tentatively, we whisper them, maybe only to ourselves or to our minister or therapist or to the "expert" on a late-night radio show. And sometimes in our despair, we cry them out loud.

Why did my child die?

Where is my child now?

Will I ever see her again?

And how do we answer such questions when they are asked of *us*? How do we talk to the friend who grieves her miscarried fetus? What meaning can she ascribe to her loss, and what happens to the souls of the unborn?

What can we say to the neighbor who confides that she speaks to her son every night? She seems relieved to be "talking" to him this way, but is it a good thing or a sign that she's in trouble?

The questions formed from our pain and the magnitude of our loss are not sensible questions, and we know it. They embarrass us and even scare us, and we're pretty sure they'll embarrass and frighten any friend we might ask them of.

Because of our limited language and because we suspect that our questions have no answers anyway, most of us don't dare to ask. Even if we were daring enough to ask an intimate friend or therapist or minister our "unreasonable" and persistent questions—"Will we be reunited when I die?" "Can I help her where she's gone?"—we wouldn't really expect an answer. They don't know; how could they know?

This lack of dialogue is peculiarly Western. In other cultures in which there is a broader language for the death of a child, there *are* answers to all these questions. They just may not be "sensible" or logical answers—at least not to us.

But logic isn't everything. Our children's deaths defy logic. When they die, the sensible part of ourselves isn't able to fathom what's happened. It may cry out its questions, but it cannot hear the answers, and if it hears, it will not comprehend. We are more than simply logical people, and our questions come from parts of ourselves other than our logical minds. They are generated out of our emotional sides, our intuitive selves, and most especially, out of our imaginations. And to these parts the answers to our urgent questions may well ring "true" and find a home beyond logic.

Of all these parts, the imagination may hold the greatest power. It can frighten and hurt us, and even strong, healthy people like Winnie are susceptible. When she imagined her grandson's violent death, she was both physically and psychologically sickened. It took her years to "get over" it, and she succeeded for the most part by avoiding the thought and, when it refused to be avoided, by forcefully, consciously turning her mind from it. She would leave her house, take a walk, grocery-shop, turn on the television, or call one of her sons or daughters or a friend.

But the same imagination that can frighten us also has the power to help us heal. Carl Simonton, M.D., Stephanie Simonton, and Martin Rossman, M.D., demonstrated this in their vanguard work with "active imagination," in which people with cancer imagined their healthy cells attacking and beating back their cancer cells.[1] Dr. Rossman has taken this approach further by successfully applying it to other diseases. These programs and many others adopted all over the United States, as well as in Europe and Latin America, have proved to be statistically significant in the treatment of various diseases and problems.

Active imagination became "visualization" and has grown to be used for everything from reducing stress to fulfilling specific goals and desires. Its effects are beneficial. I believe that opening our mind's eyes and our hearts to the power of our imagination will also affect us kindly when the subject is our children's death. This is how it works in many other cultures in which bereaved friends and family of a child who has died ask the same profound questions that our minds and our hearts and our spirits insist on asking when our children die.

In Brazil, Bali, Sulawesi, West Africa, and India, the answers, sometimes soothing, sometime evocative, sometimes challenging, have one thing in common: they each turn the attention *from the ones who have lost a child to the child who has departed.* In these places when parents ask, "Why did our child die?" they are asking for information about the *child's* fate, *his* destiny, *his* time, and sometimes *his* choice. When we cry out for the same information, we are more often really wondering what went wrong and, in many cases, what *we* did wrong.

While the details in these foreign places concerning the fate of children after death are various and sometimes contradictory, they address many of the same issues and questions that we care about here. And except in the rarest of cases, they do not allow for such feelings as the seventh guilt—*parents and siblings and closest friends do not assume responsibility for the death of a child.*

These are social systems, belief systems, religious systems, and cultures in which the people do *not* identify with God as we do. Although the relationship with spirits or gods—and there are many—is one of respect, appeasement, fear, love, and worship, the people do not confuse themselves with their gods. The lines between human beings and the miraculous powers of the immortals are deeply drawn. In such societies, while the death of a child is still tragic, it is not accompanied by the seventh guilt, the unutterable possibility or feeling that those who loved the child most are in some ineffable way responsible for that child's death.

When the identification with God is absent or broken, questions we could not answer become answerable, and possibilities we could not imagine become imaginable, and these are what we look at in Part Two.

Many of the world views we explore in Part Two will require that we "suspend disbelief," as American philosopher and psychologist William James asked us to do when examining new possibilities. As you read on, try not to weigh the foreign customs and beliefs you'll meet against the measure of logic; allow them instead to engage your feelings, your intuition, and your imagination. For these are all healing stories for the broken heart, not for the logical mind. Look for those possibilities that resonate with you and ask only, "What if these were my beliefs?" and "What if it were true?"

CHAPTER FIVE

Why Did My Child Die?

Destiny and the Seventh Guilt

Myra and Robert were desperate to understand *why* their daughter, Sara, died. "Massive trauma to the brain" was what they were told. It was not a satisfactory answer.

Why her? Why then? Why that way? Why at all? These were not logical questions, and they demanded answers way beyond the physical evidence, way beyond what the autopsy revealed.

We take these kinds of greater-than-logical questions to our counselors, our ministers, rabbis, priests, or closest friends, but their answers are often general and do not touch what we are desperate to know when our children die. The priest says we can never know God's design. The rabbi says we need to have faith that our child is at peace. Our friends may not have any words to comfort us, or they may say that time will heal our wounds. But all these answers require that we have faith, and the death of our children often shatters that, and without it we return to the question Why? And no answer satisfies.

Elsewhere this is not the case. If Myra and Robert were native Nigerians and they needed to know *why* their child had died, they would probably consult a *babalawo,* a "father of secrets" among the Yoruba, one of the largest ethnic groups in West Africa.

The *babalawos* are the general equivalent of our priests or rabbis—

spiritual counselors and teachers—but they are also diviners who "unravel the mysteries of life and death." as our senior researcher writes. The *babalawos* take their greatest questions, like "Why did this child die?" to the primary Yoruba god, Ifa.

In this culture the *babalawo* would meet with Myra and Robert and then consult the Ifa Oracle, a written text as central to the Yoruba's religion as our Bible. They might learn that it had been Sara's choice, made before her birth, to die on the day she did. The *babalawo* would describe how Sara's spirit had knelt in front of the Creator and made such decisions as what gender it would assume, which family it would be born to, and precisely how long it would live.

She could have chosen to die as a fetus or at birth, on the third or eighth day after birth, or at any time in childhood. Sometimes children die to test us, the *babalawo* would say, to see how we respond to losing them before they decide to return for a complete life.

But it is also true that a child who has chosen beforehand to live a full life may be thwarted by an accidental death, as well as by natural and even supernatural causes, and in this case the *babalawo* could tell if it were so. If it were the case, then the child would be eager to return in order to complete her interrupted life, and the family of the deceased child could look forward to her rebirth, often within a year after the initial loss.

The *babalawo* would tell Sara's parents how they would recognize her returned: "Such a child exhibits strange behaviors to prove that she is not just starting life as a day-old child. She grows rapidly, walks quickly, grows teeth earlier than scheduled, talks maturely at a tender age."

In their consultation, the family whose child has died is not focused inward on their loss, their sorrow, their pain. The *babalawo* moves them to look outside themselves, at their child's past choices and future path. And looking out at their child's agreement with the Creator, they do not assume responsibility for it; they do not insert themselves between the

Creator and the child; and they do not experience what I refer to as the seventh guilt, that guilt of false responsibility so intimately associated with our identification with God.

The Yoruba people are not the only ones who find the solution to why their children have died in their children's distant histories and who therefore spend their period of mourning focused outwardly—on the deceased child. The Yakurr, rain forest dwellers in southeastern Nigeria, say that when the child dies, his spirit remains near his body until the burial ceremonies are over. The spirit listens to comments made about it, and based on these comments, he may decide to come back to the same family and continue with the life he had begun or to change it dramatically—choose a new family and a new road entirely. The Yakurr elder would assure a couple like Myra and Robert that if the child is impressed that her parents really want her back, she will return quickly to her mother—and if this is not possible because the mother is past child-bearing age, the child will return in a short time to a close relative.

I put the question "Why does a child die?" to our senior researcher for Spiritist beliefs, one of the most widespread spiritual systems in Brazil, whose doctrine is based in part on the existence and survival of consciousness. He spoke to me of his own young son's death eighteen years earlier, as he might have spoken to Myra and Robert, explaining the Spiritist understanding of individual "life plans":

Life plans are designed with the purpose of helping a soul acquire certain understanding, overcome moral deficiencies, or assist another person's progress. Though I am not sure about the precise elements of my child's plan, I would like to think that the few years he lived here served to complete a small task left unfinished from the past, or that his soul needed the immersion in the flesh in order to receive from us, his parents, certain values or sentiments.

It is also possible that his short journey was an act of pure love with the intent of bringing his mother and father closer together, to awaken us to our own spirituality, to inspire us and his other relatives to become more generous or more forgiving.

The Spiritists believe that each life plan has a few broad, clearly established elements—time of birth, time and form of death, certain physical capabilities, place and family of birth, and dominant vocation—and that the rest is consequence of the forces and circumstances of life and of free will.

If Myra and Robert were Hindu parents in India needing to know why their child died, they might turn to a reputable astrologer. While the *babalawo* in Nigeria consults with the Ifa Oracle, and the Spiritists look to a formalized doctrine, the astrologer in India charts the exact placement of the planets at the time of the child's birth and death, noting in particular the planetary influences on the eighth house, ruler of the life-force elements of gender, birth, and death.

By interpreting these astrological maps, the astrologer in India predicts a child's life and death and even her life after death, for the position of the planets tells where the spirit will reside until it is reborn. In this tradition as well, the answers we would receive to "Why did our child die?" would turn our focus away from the empty place inside us and toward our departed children outside us and to the vast, starry mystery of life beyond our knowing.

The Concept of Destiny

As different as their disciplines and their methods, as different as their various explanations, the Ifa diviner, the Yakurr elder, the Spiritist teacher, and the Hindu astrologer would be talking to Sara's parents about Sara's destiny, a multifaceted, multidimensional, basic, determining ingredient of all life in Africa, India, and many other places throughout the world.

Unlike the people of many other countries and cultures, most Westerners do not believe in the power or effect of destiny, though it is not a totally foreign concept: classical literature like Homer's *Iliad* and *Odyssey* is all about destiny. But we don't take those lessons into our contemporary lives. Mostly we believe in the power of a good education and the effect of a strong work ethic on our future prospects. In America we teach all our grade-school children about Abraham Lincoln, who was raised in a log cabin and grew up poor and nonetheless became our sixteenth president. In this great land of opportunity, we tell our children, this could be your future. It's up to you.

No matter what our race, religion, gender, or economic status, we are taught that we can achieve anything by working at it, by not giving up. Like the Little Engine That Could, we know that if we think we can and think we can and really, really try, we will succeed at whatever we put our minds to.

To believe in destiny or fate means to believe in one possibility only. In the West we believe in many possibilities. To subscribe to destiny is to believe that our lives are predetermined. We believe in self-determination. We know that we can change and shape ourselves and make something better of our lives. We're not destined to be neurotic because of our neurotic mothers. We're not fated to make the wrong choices in our relationships. "Self-improvement" is our middle name.

We think that surrendering to the force of destiny means abandoning our belief in independence, and we Westerners are aggressively independent. Believing in destiny seems to defeat the idea of opportunity, and in America our land of opportunity is a point of national pride.

Thinking that there is some greater plan plays havoc with our notion of personal responsibility. And we so much *want* to be responsible in every area of our lives.

The Idea of Destiny as Antidote
to the Seventh Guilt

In societies that are less influenced than we are by science and psychology, the belief in destiny—its power, its inescapability, its determining role in all aspects of life and death—is widespread. People who believe that their child was *destined* to die on a certain day at a certain time under certain circumstances, although bereaved, do not necessarily feel personally *responsible* for the child's death.

If we could embrace the concept of destiny and, at least to some degree, surrender our identification with God and our passionate attachment to the power of our own wills, the enormous weight of what we believe to be our liability might be lifted and with it the eroding effects of the seventh guilt.

If my client Winnie had been raised in a religion or culture that embraced the force of destiny, she would have understood that her grandson Seth and his young wife were bound to die when they did—that it was their fate to die as they did. Although Winnie might still ask the question Why?—why was it their destiny to die so young? Why so brutally?—she would not be haunted by the possibility that she had caused their tragedy because of her own lack of diligence. She would not be asking, "How did I fail them?" Her questions would be directed at the newlyweds' fate, not at herself. She would be looking outward for her answers, toward Seth and Jill, toward their beyond and even their distant past, but not inward, as we are accustomed to doing in our psychologically inspired way of grieving.

If Myra and Robert had not been raised as rationalists, as intellectuals, perhaps even they might be open to the idea of Sara's having fulfilled her destiny rather than having been deprived of one. It was the only possibility that never came up in our therapy sessions.

The idea of destiny is not necessarily reasonable or logical, but what if it were true? Then Sara didn't die before her time; she died on the day she was supposed to. And the same would be true of Daniel's twin boy, Jesse, who may have been meant to live only a very short life.

Olivia's Purpose

As in India and Africa, many people in Latin America also believe in destiny. People who admit destiny into their lives love their children no less and mourn them as deeply as we do, but I have seen the acceptance of fate radically change the experience of a parent's grief. This was true for Rosaria, a Chilean woman, who was forty-three when she became pregnant with Olivia after three miscarriages in as many years.

A more wanted second child never existed. This time, when it seemed the baby would come to term, her parents allowed themselves the pleasure of preparing for her arrival. They bought lavishly: a lace and beribboned bassinet, tiny dresses, baby toys, bottles, booties, mobiles and rattles, diapers and flannel sheets and embroidered T-shirts. They talked to the baby, planned for the baby, dreamed of the baby. They prepared their six-year-old for big-brotherhood.

Olivia was born two months early. She weighed less than two pounds and had many severe physical complications, and it was clear that she would not survive. Although the nurses tried to remove the infant from their arms, Olivia's parents clung to her.

In spite of the nurses, Rosaria held her, and her father held them both. They drank in the sight of their beautiful, black-haired, perfectly formed, tiny, tiny daughter. They held her and never took their eyes off her, as if memorizing every feature, for the eleven minutes she lived and for some minutes longer. Finally they allowed a young nurse to take Olivia away.

Afterward, Rosaria fell into a deep depression. After some months a friend put her in touch with a woman she said might help her.

Rosaria met with the woman, who said she would try to contact

Olivia's spirit. Rosaria had not expected anything like that, but as she described it, she lacked the energy to object. Then she told me exactly what the woman reported, word for word: "Olivia says she was born for only one purpose. She says, 'I needed once, *and only once,* to truly be beheld.' "

These words hit Rosaria like a bolt of lightning. If her child had come just to be seen, surely she had gotten exactly what she desired. Rosaria's darkest days of grieving ended when she understood Olivia's destiny and believed that she had helped Olivia achieve it. She continued to miss her child. She would continue to mourn for a long time. But the possibility that her daughter had had a purpose and had fulfilled her purpose provided this mother a way to understand her child's death, if not with her logical mind, then with her heart.

It is true that people who are raised with the concept of destiny feel some of the very same conflicted emotions we do in the face of a child's death. Rosaria and her husband were as helpless as Daniel had been to prevent Jesse's dying. They were as brokenhearted, and they felt the same cavernous emptiness, but in their deepest hearts they knew that they were blameless as to cause. They did not experience the seventh guilt.

A Misty Morning on the Burning Ghats

Karma is the word that Hindus use when they speak of destiny, which includes the concept that we bear the effects of our actions in the past and that our present actions affect our future. No people are more explicit about karmic complexities and karmic justice than the Hindus, and none more eloquent, perhaps, than the Mahapatras, outcast Brahmans who perform the death rituals for bereaved families and care for the corpse and then the spirit of the deceased for ten days after cremation.

The Mahapatras are considered untouchable by much of Indian society because they are believed to carry the shadow of death. I spoke to a Mahapatra on a misty morning on the burning ghats, the wide stairway to the holy river Ganges, where bodies lay smoldering, bound tightly in thin pastel cloth on biers of bound lumber or scrap wood or branches eerily like those Abraham had laid Isaac on in my childhood coloring book. The Mahapatra himself might have been a character out of some ancient text, with his gnarled hands and wild white hair and ragged dhoti.

Most Indians I met spoke some English, but this elderly man spoke it elegantly. I asked him the same question that every family that has ever come to me grieving a lost child has asked me in one way or another: "Why does a child die?" He didn't hesitate to answer:

> A child dies either because of some sin it committed in a past life or because of some sin it has "inherited" from the father's or mother's extended bloodline.
>
> We believe that the good and bad deeds of one's past get inherited down the line. These inherited sins and merits are what account for what you call good and bad luck in this life. The modern concept of genetic diseases is, in fact, an affirmation of this Hindu belief, because disease results from sin and sin remains in the body till it gets purged. The more "intractable" sins cannot be purged in one lifetime, and the most intractable require all of *seven generations*.

This is the reason that Hindus traditionally do not intermarry, the Mahapatra said. If a man and woman are both carrying the sins of their shared ancestors as far back as seven generations, there is the potential for any child they might conceive to inherit a dangerously high concentration of bad karma.

A person's karma is visible in his astrological chart: inauspicious planetary placement is understood to be indicative of sins from previous lives, the individual's or one of his ancestor's, which have not yet been paid for. From a Western perspective, we might assume that this belief would be a source of guilt for the family of a child who dies. And yet in India there is a popular saying, "Those whom God loves die young," because it is understood that childhood death almost always lays the ground for a better next life.

The Balinese say the same: "Drastically speaking, the younger a child dies, the better it is for its soul. Life is considered punishment for the soul. That is why babies cry when they are born. They don't want to reenter another circle of life."

I was thinking of all those people I knew who had lost children or who were affected by the loss of a child when I asked the Mahapatra if there was any recourse to destiny. He waggled his head back and forth as he answered.

> Gods and goddesses can be successfully interceded with to prolong the life of a child, but whether doing so is the right thing or not is debatable! Such "successful intercessions" merely postpone the child's (and the parents') karma, you see. Parents will have to suffer such a bereavement in some future birth if not this one, and the child is not being "saved," either. Sadly, she will die in the same manner in a future birth unless her actions in this life are *extremely* meritorious, enough to cancel the karma involved. Wise parents— and they are *extremely* few—do not "mortgage" their child's future by postponing it unnecessarily.

Eliana's Story

From Brazil, Eliana is someone for whom the idea of destiny was not traditional, but she was able to connect to it on an other-than-rational level, and it definitely helped her. I met her at a dinner party in Rio. She was a professor of psychology at a major university, about my own age.

When I told her what I was working on—my research into after-death belief systems—she said she knew something about that subject. She had lost a son twenty-one years earlier and been introduced to aspects of Spiritist beliefs that had helped her through a difficult time.

The Spiritist belief system is based primarily on a world view developed in the nineteenth century by the European Allan Kardec that includes the continuous progress of the spirit, reincarnation, and a life of active service to humanity. Spiritists have a rich and detailed map of realities beyond this one. They believe in another world with many cities where people go after death according to their spiritual needs. Within these cities are all the amenities with which to carry out normal life: schools, nurseries, marketplaces, hospitals, even orphanages for children who have died.

Eliana and I met a second time for a private interview. I asked permission to record our conversation, and she agreed.

Carlos was twelve years old, almost thirteen—it was February 19—when he was hit by a car. He died on February 25. At the end of everything they told me his brain was dead from the beginning, but he was still alive for six days.

I was at the hospital very often, but I couldn't stay with him. He was at the intensive care unit, so I couldn't get in there all the time. I was at the house when they called and told me that he died.

I was desperate. My first reaction was I can't see him in a coffin, I can't, it's impossible! I was on the fourth floor of the house; he was downstairs, and I wouldn't go down to look at him and be with him. Lots of people were coming up and talking to me and telling me that I had to face it, and I couldn't do it, I couldn't.

In the middle of the night, a young girl who was the daughter of my ex-husband's sister came to see me. She was not related to me. She was about eighteen years old. I'd never respected her; she was a very young, a silly girl in my image of her, and we were not close. She was beginning to go to Spiritist sessions, and she was very enthusiastic about it. And she started to talk to me about it.

I had never heard of these beliefs. My family was Brazilian Catholic, which means not at all religious. I went to an American Protestant school. I never had any religious training when I was a child, I never prayed. But she began to talk to me about what they believe. About destiny. That Carlos was an old spirit, that he had been through many lives and that he had nothing left to do here anymore. I can't tell you the words, but she was talking to me, and I don't know why, when there were so many others whom I respected whose words of consolation or explanation had made me feel crazy, but listening to her, suddenly the whole thing started to make sense.

She told me that I had to say good-bye to him and that I shouldn't cry so much because he was following his way and this was his way. She told me he was dead because there was no need for him to be alive anymore because he was an old spirit, a wise person.

Eliana paused. "He really *was* a very wise, exceptionally wise boy, like an old spirit," she said, and she departed from her account of that evening's conversation with her niece to tell me a little about her son. They'd had an apartment on a beach in Guarujá, where they spent their summers, and Carlos had had many friends among the boys who "worked" the beach, selling peanuts and trinkets to the tourists—poor boys from poor families. One night Eliana arrived home late to find Carlos waiting up for her.

He didn't want me to be alarmed that there was a boy sleeping in his room. He told me not to worry because the boy was clean. He had had the boy take a bath and given him a pair of pajamas before he went to bed. He invited him because his mother was a prostitute and he slept on the beach while his mother was working with men in the house. "So if you don't mind, I want him to sleep here," he told me.

So you see why I say he seemed like a wise soul, someone wiser than the average ten-year-old.

Then she shared something that gave me chills. The day her son was struck by the car that killed him was the last day of their vacation. That morning Carlos had dropped a note on Eliana's breakfast tray. Eliana reached into her purse and handed it to me. The paper was as soft as cloth, and the ink faded. She read it in English, translating for me: "I have the best house in the world. I am the happiest child in the world. I have the most wonderful swimming pool and the best mother in the world."

I showed this to my niece that night. She said, "Isn't it as if he knew? As if he wanted to leave you something? Won't you go down and thank him for that?" It made sense to me, and suddenly I could go down and see him and talk to him. I talked to him until the last moment. I didn't go to the cemetery, but I was very close to him. I thanked him and I said good-bye.

Had Eliana been the same highly accomplished professor of psychology but American, her story might have had a different focus. Eliana would more likely have castigated herself for not having broken down the doors of intensive care to be with her son, for not having been with him when he died. She might have blamed herself for her inability to sit with her son after his death or for not attending his funeral or for not "picking up" on the deeper implication of Carlos's last words of love.

Eliana suffered. I do not mean to belittle the depth of her loss. Here we were twenty-one years later, still feeling it. But Eliana did not take Carlos's death on herself. She missed him, but she did not believe on any level that she had been responsible for his death.

She tried to pursue the Spiritist teachings. A student of hers at the university invited her to attend classes at the Spiritist training center in São Paulo, and she went a few times, she said.

> But I'm not a religious person. I couldn't follow the whole thing, the astral cities and so forth. The details were too hard for me to accept, and then I gave up.
>
> But if you ask me what I believe, I do believe that we live many lives. I do believe that he didn't need to be alive anymore. He went away because that was his destiny—or the time he had to be here. It made sense to me. I still believe it.

For so many of us stuck in a world where rationality and responsibility rule, the death of a child does not make "sense" unless someone is guilty, and then we may engage in a lifetime struggle with feelings of blame and shame.

But what if there were such a thing as destiny? In worlds where life and death are part of a great cycle or part of a greater plan than we mortals can know, we would still weep, still ache, still grieve for our children who are gone—but we would not say, "In some way I am responsible." And that makes all the difference in the world.

CHAPTER SIX

Where Is My Child Now? Will I Ever See Him Again?

Life After Death, a Counterforce to Freezing in Time

The way we look at time has a profound effect on how we perceive life. In the modern West we think of time as a commodity, something finite and limited. We think of life the same way.

We have a certain amount of time in which to live. Our lives are supposed to have a beginning, a middle, and an end. When our children die in what we perceive as the beginning or the middle of their lives, we believe that they have been robbed of their birthright—the right to those three stages. They've run out of time, we say. Their time is up too soon. We could as easily substitute the word *life* for *time*. They've run out of life; their life is up too soon.

In cultures in which life is a continuum and time is not something you run out of or use up, death does not signify the irreconcilable end of all life and all experience. Death is more an event, a space, a separation, followed usually by a resting period (for children the resting period is usually shorter than for an adult) and then new life. And this cycle is unending.

Our understanding of time is a major cause of our impulse to freeze our children after death. On some deep psychological level, we are trying to keep them with us; on another, we hope to keep them safe this way. We don't know exactly what happens to them when they leave us and our time frame, and we fear what we don't know. Freezing the child is an effort to preserve what is known—known time, known place, known child. But freezing the child does not help her or keep her safe.

We are not entirely unlike the cultures we have been looking at. We share a belief in the existence of human "spirit." Most of us say that the spirit continues even after the body dies, and most of us conceive of an afterlife.[1] But here is where the similarities between our beliefs and those of many, many other cultures cease.

Most of us consider that after a quick trip, heaven is the end of evolution for our child. Jesse may be surrounded by angels, but he's not going anywhere from there. He won't grow up to be an adult. He'll always be not yet four years old. When our children die, we may freeze them in heaven just as we do in our hearts and in our homes.

Good Heavens

A recent *Time* magazine poll declared that 81 percent of Americans believe in heaven (defined as "where people live forever with God after they die"), but *Time*'s front-page story "Does Heaven Exist?" opens: "It used to be that the hereafter was virtually palpable, but American religion now seems almost allergic to imagining it. Is paradise lost?"[2]

Although people say they believe in heaven, they aren't clear anymore about what that means. "Where did he really go?" is a question I have heard from almost every grieving parent.

Some years ago I had a client whose eight-year-old became terribly upset when his parents planted a tree to mark the first anniversary of his older sister's death. Eventually his father found the root of the boy's withdrawal, temper tantrums, and bed wetting. Where exactly was his sister? he wanted to know. Was she in the box in the ground in the cemetery, where he *saw* them put her? Or was she with God, as they said she was? Or was her spirit living in the new tree? And would she move again?

The child believed that he might lose track of his sister's whereabouts, that he wouldn't be able to find her if he needed to. Not knowing where she was confused and frightened him.

We Westerners don't have any consensus about where heaven is "really" or what goes on there. Our "concept of exactly what it is has grown foggier, and [we] hear about it much less frequently from [our] pastors," says *Time*.[3] And this loss has hurt us considerably, according to Peter Kreeft, professor of philosophy at Boston College and author of *Everything You Ever Wanted to Know About Heaven . . . but Never Dreamed of Asking*. Having lost the details of what it means to reside in heaven, Kreeft maintains, has diminished "our sense of beauty, glory, wonder, awe, magnificence, triumph" and turned our contemplation of life after death into something "joyless."[4]

In places where paradise has not been "lost," the death of a child is still painful for the family and friends of that child, but there is immeasurable comfort in having a clear image of the afterworld, a definitive answer to the question "Where did he really go?"

The Spiritists of Brazil tell us, for example, that when the child dies, rescue teams composed of the child's own family from generations past come to meet him. They cut the ties that the child's spirit has to his earth family, and take him to an appropriate institution, given his particular evolutionary path and special needs.

If we applied Spiritist beliefs in the case of Daniel's twin boy, Jesse, for instance, he would wake up in the spiritual realm, much like anyone who returns from a long period under anesthesia. At first he would have only a vague sense of the light filtering into his room, the Spiritists might say, a place that in its smallest details resembled precisely his own room at home, with its toy trucks and coloring books.

Sometimes the child awakens in a hospital room if that is the more familiar environment. This was so for the child of our Spiritist senior researcher, who described for me where he believed his son had gone after death.

> My boy was taken into a Spiritist community hospital that is equipped to bring the person along without shock. It may have taken several days (in our calendars) for him to recover his full self-awareness. Though it is incredible for the average person on earth, this picture is very plausible when we think that this simulated environment is sculpted with the forces of the mind. It's like thinking of creations in a virtual reality space.

In this next world, in a clean white hospital or a fully equipped, state-of-the-art intensive care unit or a "first care" unit in one of the sparkling spiritual cities that sit above our earthly material ones, the defective valve in Jesse's heart would be mended.

Then, a Spiritist would assure his parents, his great-grandparents would take Jesse home to live with them for a while in their cozy house in a light-filled neighborhood. Jesse would grow up a little in this other world, go to school, make friends, have a life—unless he reincarnated very quickly after he was well. In that case, he might leave the hospital for an orphanage that provided every comfort and every plaything a child could want. He might enroll in a reincarnation program to help him prepare for returning. Normally he would soon be reborn into his old family, if not to Evelyn, then to a relative of hers or of Daniel's.

The Idea of Life After Death as the Other Side of Freezing

In the same way that a belief in destiny can help to eliminate the terrible effects of the guilt that says we are responsible for our child's death, the idea of return can soften the hard edged pain of separation that we respond to by freezing our children in time. While not its opposite, reincarnation is the other side of freezing. Freezing stops time; accepting reincarnation extends it.

If we can envision our children coming into our lives for a while, bestowing their blessings or achieving their purpose, and then continuing on in a longer or another life journey, we are less likely to freeze them at the time of their death. And by not holding them back from what the future holds for them, we release ourselves to what the future may hold for us.

What if it were true? What if, as the Spiritists say, there were another world, complete with marketplaces, movie theaters, schools, hospitals, city streets, quiet neighborhoods, and families and friends, where our children are being cared for after death? And what if we tried to imagine it? What if we put our minds to exploring these sparkling "astral cities" and tried to picture the architecture and the landscape and began to fill in the details of what this place might be like?

We need not become Spiritists to do this. But doesn't it help enormously to have all these details, to wonder about such a possibility, to think about our children's existence in such a place? I believe that if my client Barbara had known precisely and in detail where her son Zach was, that he was all right and was with friends and family, and that he might finish reading the book he left behind—and that he might return somehow, somewhere—she would not have been compelled to sit weeping for so long in the memorial room she kept for him at home.

Our senior researcher for the Spiritists told me more about his son's reception in his afterlife:

I know that Marcus was greeted by Grandma Clar, the person I would entrust him with without hesitation. My wife and I often hear accounts of his life in the spirit world: we know that he was taken in by her and other family members. Our family had always been very close. My father, who died over thirty-five years ago, would be there, and he would argue stubbornly to be master coordinator of a special reunion. That was his style, and I did not expect him to change in the spirit world. This was comforting. My boy would not be left alone, thrown into some scary place. Nor would he have to be in pain or in tears or in shock without his teddy bear. Their immense love for him was a solace.

I think that the father who turned down a deanship at an eastern college because it meant moving away from the home his daughter grew up in might have made a different choice if he could have imagined her safe in a home of her own.

We freeze our children in known time and known place when we don't know where they are. Who cares for our children where they have gone? Are they with their grandparents? Do they have a life beyond this one that we can understand? Today I encourage my clients to steep themselves in imagining the afterworld, to ask their minister or rabbi or priest for explicit descriptions of life after death, to picture a life as full and rich as they can for their children now. For this is the way people in other places find solace when their children pass out of their world—not by freezing them in a familiar time and place but by imagining them in a well-defined world after.

Returning for a Visit

There is another reason we often resort to freezing our children after death. We don't believe that we will ever be with them again otherwise. We don't believe they'll ever return to us in this life. But the understanding that after death the spirit may return to life on earth is basic to people with a multidimensional experience of time, and reincarnation is a fundamental belief in many, if not most, other cultures. We are a minority in the West who do not share this belief.

There seem to be two basic worldwide understandings of how our children return to us: in one the spirit resides permanently in the after-world but comes back periodically for brief visits to loved ones; in the second the spirit resides only temporarily in the afterworld and comes back for a lifetime. In Mexico the celebration of the Day of the Dead every early November is an example of the former, with departed spir-its returning for a day of feasting and festivities at their grave sites. Chil-dren return to the world on the first night of the holiday; other departed family and friends come back on the second. They say you can tell when the children's spirits have arrived by the flickering of the long tapered candles that adorn their graves, a signal that they are partaking of the essences of candies and cookies that have been prepared for them. The Maya celebrated a similar week-long ritual in which the children ar-rived on the morning of October 31 and departed on November 7. On the last day the candles were lit again on the graves of the children "so that the 'angels' may see their road."[5]

In Brazil I attended an Umbanda ritual for summoning the spirits of dead children for visits that last less than an hour but may occur as often as once or twice a week. In many other systems, however, the "visits" back to earth are the length of another life. (The Umbanda ritual is de-scribed in Chapter 9, "Calling the Children.")

Returning for Another Life

Most of the cultures that accept the idea of continuous time understand that life repeats itself on earth as a series of reincarnations, each one mov-ing the spirit closer to perfection or completion or an idyllic forever-more. Very often these reincarnations occur within the same family. The Tlingit Indians of the American Northwest believe it is possible to influ-ence their return to their own family by expressing that desire before death.[6] The Hopi Indians believe that a child who dies returns to the parental house and waits to be reborn into the body of the next child. A boy reappears as a girl, and vice versa. If no other child is born before the mother dies, the spirits of her dead children meet her after death to accompany her to the underworld.[7]

The Ojhas, a class of shamans in India, speak about a complicated phenomenon referred to as "single-minded births." If a son or daughter has neglected or mistreated his or her parent, the parent may take revenge after death by being reborn to the abusive offspring. After exacting the love and nurturance they feel they are owed, these reborn parents will die in infancy or early childhood.

To us, on this side of time, the death of a child may look like life interrupted, but on another side of time, as the Ojha shaman sees it, the same event marks a kind of poetic completion.

There are many different understandings of how many times we return. Some Spiritists say that we come back to this world three times or three-and-a-fraction-more times. If there is one small piece of information a person still needs to complete his time on earth, he uses that fraction more of life—a child's portion—to find it. This is what accounts for the deaths of children.

Hindus and many Buddhists believe we return as many times as we have unfinished business to settle or karma to pay. The Fon, numerically the most significant ethnic group of the Benin Republic of Africa, say that the *only* souls that come back for another life on earth are those of children who die, and they always come back because they cannot achieve their destination in the afterworld until they complete a full life.

Traditional birth attendants in Nigeria also tell us that we can and do see our dead children again. It is the common belief among the Yoruba women of southwestern and northern Nigeria, as well as among the Igbo of eastern Nigeria, that a child does not completely abandon her parents in spirit when she dies. "This is about the living dead," one of these wise women explained, "and it gives hope to a mother who at one time or the other has lost her child but knows that the spirit of the dead child will come as a living child and be grafted back to the family."

Children Who Are Born to Die

In those countries where an individual spirit chooses its own destiny, there is another fascinating aspect to reincarnation that applies specifically to children who are believed to be born to die. The Yoruba call such children *abiku.* In these cases the same child is reborn over and over again into the same family.

In African states where infant mortality is high, it is not uncommon for a woman to deliver ten or more babies who die at birth or in infancy. Where we might consider such a mother to be a victim of repeated miscarriages or infant deaths, the Yoruba would know she was dealing with an *abiku,* a child born to die.

When they are not in utero or spending their short time on earth, the *abiku* reside as adolescents in an extraterrestrial world, Ajiran, also called "near-heaven," located between heaven and earth very near the African city Ile-Ife, which is believed to be the cradle of the human race and perhaps the lost city of Atlantis. Ajiran is distinguished from the physical universe by the thinnest line of demarcation.

They say that openings to this near-heaven exist around garbage dumps, on plantain plantations, in riverbank areas, in thick jungles, or at crossroads. At these places the *abiku* gather. They hang out together like the teenage gangs we have here. They wait in trees (the *lobgokiyan* tree is a particular favorite), and at midnight or midday they steal into the wombs of pregnant mothers, displacing the souls who would have been born. For this reason pregnant Yoruba women rarely go out at noon or late at night, and they avoid places where *abiku* might be waiting.

Just as we call in a specialist if our baby is ill, parents in many African villages call for a diviner to tell if their child is *abiku,* born to die. Often it is all too obvious.

If the new child is an *abiku,* he may bear the same or similar scars or birthmarks as a child who has recently died in the family or the community. If he was formerly lame, deaf, mute, or mentally deficient, he may return handicapped or impaired.[8] He may be born with the same number of teeth as he died with. He may retain gender and complexion. He will cry, eat, and sleep in the same postures as the previous baby did. He will assume former expressions and behaviors that anyone who knew him previously will recognize. Sometimes such children act strangely or erratically. Some *abiku* children provide vivid eyewitness accounts of their previous life that can be confirmed by third parties. And it is said that *abiku* are often more intelligent than other children, demonstrating a supernatural familiarity with life on earth.

Parents attempt to defeat the *abiku*'s spirit "companions" by giving their child a terrible name like Aja (Dog) or Omolasan (Just a Stupid Child) so that his afterlife companions will turn away from him when he comes to rejoin them. Rituals are performed and sacrifices made, and medical interventions are sought in order to keep the child in the earthly realm, alive and healthy. But there is a Yoruba expression, "The *abiku* makes a liar of the doctor," and all too often the child is not saved.

When the child dies in spite of all precautions, its corpse may be marked with ash; it may even be severely mutilated in order to make it so offensive to its spirit gang that they will not want it back. Fear of the power of *abiku* and concern for surviving siblings are so strong that the surviving brothers and sisters may also be cut so they are hard for the *abiku* spirit to recognize should he come for them.

The *abiku* are said to be absolutely loyal to one another. They vow always to return to their spirit society in near-heaven. Some say that no matter what sacrifices are made by the unfortunate family of such a child to keep that child alive, the *abiku* will prevail. But I have spoken to diviners who claim to have been successful in diverting the *abiku,* and it is more generally believed that an *abiku* child can be "chained permanently to the world" if one makes the necessary sacrifices and appeases its companions in the spiritual realm. There are even stories of diviners making "parting agreements" with *abiku* children, offers to make it more appealing for the born-to-die child to break its contract with its spirit companions in exchange for a reward of money or privilege if it will stay. In some cases, I am told, it works.

An Abiku's Own Story

Like many Africans, Oyenike wore her tribal markings on her face—three vertical lines on three horizontals. She was in her late forties, of light complexion, and she walked with a limp. Her left leg was half paralyzed. She had just delivered at a traditional birth clinic located at Abimbola village in Osun state and was there for her five-day stay as a nursing mother when she confided to her traditional birth attendant that she was an *abiku*. Her personal history was recorded by the attendant:

> Any *abiku* that grows to maturity should be able to remember her childhood days as an *abiku*. Spirit children are gifted in knowing what has happened to them, what will happen later in life, and even when they will die.
>
> I came to the world as a male at first birth and came as a female at subsequent births. I belonged to a group of seven born-to-die children. Each of us owed allegiance to the group and would not fail to execute any program that we had to perform while we were living children.
>
> We used to make pledges—trying to outdo one another in mischief—such as making an old woman our first mother, dying as a fetus, coming as a stillbirth, dying on the eighth-day naming ceremony, or dying on a marriage day or other memorable occasion. We were terrible!
>
> No amount of traditional charm, medicine, or aid could make us stay longer than the chosen period. We died and lived according to the oaths made with our gang. . . .

After every death, as a spirit, I followed my mother everywhere. Whenever she consulted with a diviner for a remedy to make me stay the next time, I would seize the sacrifices the diviner prescribed and throw them away or render them useless. Sometimes my gang in near-heaven would eat the edible sacrifices just to convince the healers, diviners, and general practitioners that we were more powerful than any of them. . . .

The only thing that can make an *abiku* stay, unless we want to, is when the mother rejects the child by mutilating its corpse. The *abiku* detest such symbols and will immediately send any member marked that way back to life and not allow him to rejoin their group.

This astonishing former *abiku* told the birth attendant that she finally decided to remain on earth to live a full life because she wanted to have children of her own. As she matured, she said, she discovered that she had an intuitive knowledge of the medicinal plants used to manage childhood diseases. She attributed this to the fact that her parents had treated her with such remedies often in her previous lives in their efforts to prevent her from dying.

The theory and the rituals that relate to the *abiku* may seem disturbing and cruel to our Western minds, but they exemplify a theme that was constantly brought home for me as I learned about other people's ways of understanding child death: in these cultures the parents do not assume personal responsibility for the deaths of their children.

Bonnie and Beatrice

According to a recent Gallup poll, 22 percent of Americans believe in reincarnation, but they do so outside most sanctioned religious systems.[9] Neither orthodox Christianity, Islam, nor popular Judaism subscribes to the idea of individual reincarnation, although I remember as a child hearing that before God sent us back down to earth, he pressed his index finger to our lips and said, "Shhh. Now don't say anything about where you've been!" And that is what accounts for the indentation just above our upper lips and the fact that we don't usually speak of previous lives and ultimately forget them.

I clearly remember the first time in my practice that the possibility of returning became a subject of conversation. I met Sherri three years after her youngest daughter died of an *E. coli* infection after drinking tainted apple juice. But Sherri had not come to see me about Bonnie's death, as I'd thought.

Sherri had become pregnant again very soon after Bonnie died and was now the mother of a beautiful two-year-old named Beatrice. With Sherri's permission and corrections, I've re-created what she told me at our first meeting.

> I know this sounds strange—the only person I've ever told this to is my sister, and she's known as the family crazy—but I have always believed that when Beatrice was born, we were not meeting for the first time.
>
> I know it's nuts. I know people would say that this is still part of my grieving for Bonnie or that I've watched too many episodes of *Twilight Zone.* I've already heard everybody's opinion about what a bad idea it was to give the baby a name with the same first initial as Bonnie. But the name similarity is really nothing compared with what races through my mind in those moments when she looks at me a certain way or reaches for the same red plush toy that Bonnie loved best of all.

Sherri showed me a current photograph of Beatrice and one of Bonnie at the same age, and the resemblance was striking. Both children had the same strawberry blonde tendrils, dark eyes, button nose, and dimples. "It's like the new baby is an echo of the old," Sherri said very quietly, and it was quite true.

I was particularly struck by her tone as she confided in me. She was not full of wonder and joy at the possibility that her daughter might have returned. She had felt obliged to offer an apologia for the strangeness of what she was going to tell me and an acknowledgment of how "nuts" it was. She sounded resigned.

> When friends and family have the courage to say how much she looks like Bonnie, I keep hoping they'll say more, but it always stops there, at genetics. My husband will have nothing to do with any of this. I've tried to broach it with him, but he says I'm getting like my crazy sister. . . .
>
> I haven't even told you about our dog, Slipper, who adored Bonnie and is totally devoted to Beatrice—has been from the moment we brought her home from the hospital. He seemed to recognize her immediately—came wagging and squealing with pleasure—he almost knocked me down to get to her. He's like a nanny, he's so devoted to her. He sleeps under the crib. And Slipper never showed any interest in any of our other children, I swear to you.
>
> It's been two years, and the similarities are more, not less. She walked very early, like her sister. And her taste in food. She gags on applesauce.

Beatrice's two older sisters, twelve and fourteen years old when Beatrice was born, agreed that the new baby was very similar to Bonnie, but Sherri had been afraid to pursue the subject with them. She seemed embarrassed to tell her story at all, as if she were ashamed of considering the possibility of her daughter's return. I asked her if this was so. She looked at me a long moment, and then she began to cry.

Sherri's relief at being able to discuss the possibility of reincarnation was the beginning of her own return to life. In subsequent meetings the tone and quality of our conversations grew livelier. Where at first she had been extremely reserved, now she became more animated.

Along with these signs of health and the return of Sherri's spirit came a kind of peaceful satisfaction in the idea of Bonnie's spirit having come back in Beatrice. I watched that good feeling turn to appreciation for the gift of Beatrice, which touched every aspect of Sherri's life over the following years, and although it remained something she kept to herself for the most part, she no longer felt either "strange" or "nuts" about allowing it to be true.

What Does Reincarnation Offer?

Ian Stevenson, M.D., of the University of Virginia has done the most extensive investigation into reincarnation and reports of claims of reincarnation among people in northern India, Sri Lanka, Burma, Thailand, south-central Turkey, Lebanon, Syria, West Africa, and northwestern North America, as well as in Europe and elsewhere in North America and, to a lesser degree, in South America.

Stevenson, who has published six scholarly works in many volumes on the subject, notes that although "evidence" for reincarnation is asserted by some people based on past-life readings, hypnotic regressions, the experience of déjà vu, dreams and nightmares, drug- or fever-induced visions, spontaneous or induced "recovered" memories, as well as phobias and aversions, affinities and attractions, he has less confidence in these than in the spontaneous, unsolicited comments of children who report in astonishing verifiable detail about previous lives.[10]

In gathering material for this book, I also heard about cases of children who seemed familiar with people, objects, and events they had never had contact with or experienced before. One of our senior researchers in Nigeria told me about a friend of his who was convinced his youngest son was actually his older son who had returned: "The child asked to be called his dead brother's name, an unusual request in that our culture does not permit children to pick their own names. Also, the boy would suddenly recount in great detail events that happened long before he was born."

The Yoruba diviners point to children who "start talking about knowing certain people in the family compound before being introduced to them . . . [who] reflect on past events, and parents wonder how they know these things."

Across cultures, the apparent ability of some children to remember past lives fades as the child ages, until by age five or seven the child rarely makes such references and eventually forgets all about them.

How many of our own children have tried to tell us about a previous life and been dismissed as talking nonsense or, worse, lying? Watching a playground full of children, Carol Bowman, author of *Children's Past Lives: How Past Life Memories Affect Your Child,* asks that question and conjectures:

> Out of the fifty, I would be surprised if there wasn't *at least* one who, when younger, began to speak of "when I lived before". . . .
>
> What I had learned about children's past life memories had changed the way I look at all children. Most adults unconsciously see children as something less than real people because the young haven't had enough life experience, haven't matured into adults yet. But if we all have had innumerable past lives, then these children zooming around in front of me could be very experienced souls, only in little bodies. I looked again at the kids on the playground, squinted my eyes, and imagined them as wise beings trapped temporarily in childhood. That made a difference. It made me want to ask each and every one of them: "Where have you been? What can you teach me?"[11]

Carol Bowman's comments reminded me of Eliana's reference to her son, Carlos, as an "old spirit," a "wise soul." "Old soul" and variations on it are phrases so frequently used by parents of children who have died that you have to wonder if there may not be something to it. The evidence for reincarnation may not qualify as "scientific" to everyone, but we are not engaged in a science lab; we are only trying to imagine What if it were so? What does the idea of reincarnation offer us when our children die?

Reincarnation offers life for the child and all of life's possibilities for that child, as opposed to incomprehensible death and loss. The idea of a continuing journey, ongoing and unending, lets us envision the measure of life as a circle that has no end rather than a straight line that does. Reincarnation tells us that neither life nor death is a terminal affair.

Maybe most hopefully, reincarnation makes reunion possible in this lifetime or in a life to come.

Where reincarnation is a foreign concept, we can see no further than our own horizons. When our child is gone from our lives, it is hard to imagine him in any other; he ceases to exist except in our minds; he isn't real anymore. Holding on to his memory, keeping it rigid, focusing intently, only fools us into believing that he is alive.

But where returning is the way of all understanding, the death of a child is different again. Here, where time is endless and not bound by the horizon, we may miss our child, but we know that he continues to be. Here we *can* imagine him in another place, with our most beloved ancestors, or in the light-filled chambers of the gods or somewhere else on earth. Here we can look forward to the possibility of seeing him again.

The imagination hungers for such radiant images and comforting thoughts when our hearts are heavy with loss. These images can take us out of ourselves, can let us follow our children's path after death—and that just may be a path that circles back to life.

CHAPTER SEVEN

Are the Unborn Real?

Death Before Life, Expanding the Language After Death

If the death of a child we love is a subject about which we do not speak because of insufficient language, we have even fewer words with which to talk about the death of the unborn. What was it that we carried and lost? We're shy about calling it a baby until it is born, and for many people the word *fetus* sticks in the throat. Yet death before life is a common occurrence. In this county more than 20 percent of all pregnancies end in miscarriage.[1]

But we are silent on all fronts about miscarriages. We don't talk about the physical details, fearful of offending our listener. We don't describe the emotional aspects because without language, we can't express them—besides, our culture rarely acknowledges that there are any emotional aspects to miscarriage. We're encouraged not to take it too seriously. It's a disappointment maybe, but not a death.

The miscarried child remains in many ways a stranger to us. We may never know its sex. We may never name it or hold it or even see it. Pregnancy usually ends before a woman is showing, so few people know, and even if they did know, they wouldn't have the language to speak of it.

For those families who lose a child in the later stages of pregnancy, or whose child is stillborn or dies at birth, the tragedy seems compounded by the fact that so many people did know—the pregnancy was obvious—and still we don't know what to say or how to help.

There are a few safe places to discuss the particular loss that women and often their husbands experience after a miscarriage or stillbirth or neonatal death, and the therapist's office is one of them.

Andrea's Story

Andrea was thirty-four years old, nearly six feet tall, a striking red-haired attorney. And she was tough as nails. She didn't see the point of therapy, but a lawyer colleague of hers had convinced her to come to see me "just once." She was here because she couldn't stop crying, she said, and began to cry.

I lost my baby three months before it should have been born. When they told me it was dead, I was shocked. But that wasn't the worst. I had to keep carrying it for another month. I was big, and people would congratulate me. What was I supposed to say? Never mind, it's dead?

I had to deliver it in the operating room like it was alive. They wanted to show it to me. Why would I want to see a dead fetus? But they took pictures and I have them. But I won't look at them.

It wasn't a real baby; it was more like a specimen. You don't bury them—they take care of that. But I feel so useless. And I can't stop crying.

Until that moment I had not heard of such a possibility—of having to carry a dead fetus to near term, of having to deliver it as if it were a baby. I, too, was shocked, and by the time Andrea finished speaking, tears were streaming down my face.

"Are you crying too?" she asked, peering at me in confusion. "Why are you crying?"

"I'm crying at what an awful thing you've been through," I said.

"But it wasn't real," she said, repeating what she had been told. "It wasn't a real baby."

"Feels like it was real," I said.

Andrea returned for a second visit. "You didn't tell me what to do," she announced as she settled into her chair.

She felt a great deal better, she told me, with apparently no curiosity as to why that might be so. She was here because she needed to *do* something. She wanted to know what she should do.

She had told me that she was brought up in an observant Catholic family. I asked her if she was comfortable in church.

"After this I don't really believe in God anymore," she said.

"But do you like being in church?"

She did, as a matter of fact. And when I asked if she knew a priest, she laughed and said that she knew many.

"Go to church and tell a priest what happened," I said. "Ask him to say a mass."

"You think that will help?"

"It can't hurt," I said.

Natalie's Story

The term *high achiever* doesn't do Natalie justice. She graduated magna cum laude in comparative literature from Stanford, received highest honors from Harvard Graduate School of Business, spoke five languages fluently, and was a world traveler. When she wasn't traveling, she designed computer software and wrote poetry.

When Natalie became pregnant at age thirty-five, her home filled with books on pregnancy, and she became an expert in this subject, as in everything else she tackled. When she lost the fetus at two-and-a-half months, she was devastated. She turned her formidable energy toward discovering why she had miscarried. She and her husband visited specialists in this country and in Europe.

Natalie believed that she was responsible for failing to bring her child to term. Her body had failed. Or her husband's had. Her self blame was fed at first by her doctors, who performed all manner of tests, looking for a biological cause.

But there was no physical reason Natalie could not have a healthy baby. Ultimately, she and her husband were assured that they probably would the next time. It's not so unusual to miscarry, Natalie learned. Just keep trying, her doctors told her. Better luck next time.

These things happen.

But Natalie was not consoled by these vague nonanswers. She felt isolated and depressed and lacking the rational means for dealing with what had happened to her. When she came to see me about her depression, I suggested that she try mourning her loss. She stiffened perceptibly.

"What loss?" she inquired with an arched eyebrow.

"The loss of your baby," I said.

"But it wasn't a baby," she explained patiently. "It was a two-and-a half-month-old fetus."

"Some people would consider it a baby," I said.

"No," Natalie said firmly. "According to Catholic doctrine, the soul is considered to enter the fetus at three months, not before."[2]

Natalie, daughter of atheists, was not Catholic; in fact, she professed to have no religious beliefs whatsoever, but of this arcane fact she was sure.

Where Language Exists
for the Unborn

One might think the pain would be less for the parents who never get to know their children, for the parents of a baby who enters the world very briefly, or for those whose child never enters the world alive at all. But it is not possible to compare the grief that families and friends endure when a loved child dies and that would-be parents may experience following a miscarriage or stillbirth or the death of a newborn.

Because our culture does not generally acknowledge life or "viability" until a child is born, it is difficult for us to acknowledge how we may be affected when, as it is believed elsewhere, our child's spirit departs before birth or at birth. That we *are* affected is not at issue, though. When I began the research for this book, I was eager to learn how other cultures deal with death before life and how they speak of it.

The first thing I discovered was an astonishingly rich language relative to the phenomenon of the unborn child. For instance, the Toraja of Sulawesi, Indonesia, consider their unborn children to be as basic a part of life as rain.

They say that the souls of stillborn children continue to roam about on earth or stay with spirits in the forest. They're always thirsty; they can hear the river murmuring but cannot find it. They feed themselves on dewdrops, which they lick off blades of grass and the leaves of trees. An unborn soul will wait in a kind of limbo until the soul of its mother comes by. Then the little soul will cling to her and let himself be taken along to the city of the dead. (It is said the infant spirits may also try to latch on to other passing souls, but these others shake the little ones off.)

Priestesses among the Toraja say that on their trips through the air they meet the souls of the stillborn and babies who died, who ask to be taken back to earth, but the priestesses must answer that it is not possible. The priestesses are deeply distressed over the fate of the little ones. They tearfully promise to celebrate a feast for the dead on the unborns' behalf.

"Then the souls stop crying, and this is to the good," it is written, "because through all this crying too much rain falls on earth, so that the crops might well fail."[3]

In addition to a language filled with such poetic imagery, other cultures have a variety of rituals that families and community members perform after miscarriages or stillbirths to help the child's spirit on its journey in the afterworld and even encourage its return. These rituals give us another layer of language.

The Karanga people of Zimbabwe, Africa, bury a premature or stillborn fetus in river sand in a *gambe*-jar, whose shape suggests a uterus. The burial is attended by women only. The uterine symbol is considered so powerful that no man may participate—a woman's sexual organs are never to be looked upon in public by a man.

During the first rain when the river rises (the river being symbolic of amniotic fluid), the *gambe*-jar with its unborn baby is swept away. At precisely the same time, the people say, that very same baby is born alive to a woman somewhere else on earth.[4]

I thought of Andrea and Natalie needing to acknowledge the reality of their unborn babies, who performed their healing rituals in private, with a therapist, as opposed to a gathering of women on a riverbank seeing a child's spirit off and *helping* that child into its next life. Along with language, our culture's acknowledgment of a woman's loss and of her need to do something for her lost child is something we are missing in the West.

In Modern Japan, a Special Relationship with the Unborn

Among all the cultures I have researched on this subject, Japan seems to have the most developed language, in our broad use of the word, for the phenomenon of death before life.

According to Japanese tradition, burial rites that ensure the spirit's passage to the afterworld are reserved for the spirits of those who have *lived* and died. The unborn baby—including the aborted fetus—is caught in a kind of limbo, disconnected from its biological family because it was not born and is denied access to the ancestral family in the afterworld because it died without living.

To prevent such a lonely fate for their unborn child, parents perform a naming ritual,[5] which makes the dead child recognizable to its ancestors, and they call on the Buddhist guardian of crossroads and transitions, whose name is Jizo, to protect and guide the unborn child across the river between this world and the next.

By securing Jizo's loving protection and ensuring the unborn soul a safe crossing to the afterworld, the parents of an aborted or miscarried or stillborn baby, even of an infant who dies very early, hope to demonstrate their devotion and encourage the child to be reborn to them soon.[6]

Jizo is represented by a statuette or effigy, usually made of stone or plastic, although some fabulously artful one-of-a-kind Jizo figures are gaining favor. They are usually one to nearly two feet high. They look like little Buddhas, with similar sweet, round faces, beatific expressions, and shaved heads.

At the same time that these figures represent the deity Jizo, they look very much like babies too, and they also symbolize the unborn child or one who died soon after birth. These children are called *mizuko,* which means literally "child of the water."[7] The reference is to the unborn children stranded on the banks of the river that separates life and death, unable to cross without Jizo's help.[8]

The practices associated with the *mizuko* are hundreds of years old. Originally the word referred exclusively to an aborted fetus. In Japan abortion is still a common means of birth control; 300,000 to 400,000 legal abortions are performed there each year.[9] But today, according to journalist Elizabeth Harrison, the word *mizuko* refers to any child who dies " 'out of order,' that is, before its parents."[10]

Mizuko jizo statues can be seen everywhere—standing along country roads and in mobs of tens of thousands at temples throughout Japan, crowding the courtyards, no longer all alone, no longer invisible. They may be dressed in a baby bonnet and bib or in an embroidered sweater. Their parents may even buy them little toys and attach them to the statues. Some of the figures wear pearls.

In private homes a *mizuko jizo* is given a position of honor, and the family offers it food and drink and changes its clothes on special occasions.

When I first learned about the custom, I wondered if it was an Eastern version of the kind of memorialization that takes place when we freeze our children in Western cultures. I found significant differences. First, unborn children in Japanese culture are understood to be on a journey, and their parents are helping them on their way, not holding them back.

Further, as a symbol of the child, *mizuko jizo* figures represent toddlers, usually older than the infant or fetus that died; old enough, according to a study published by Princeton University Press, to "interact in a variety of ways, including playing with would-be parents and being aware of the parents' feelings. . . . Regret can be expressed to a child who would have been."[11]

Could the Japanese "regret" over their unborn children be anything like that terrible feeling of responsibility that we are calling the seventh guilt? I wondered. Again I found a difference. In Japan the regret over a miscarried or stillborn child, even over an aborted fetus, is for the possibility of consigning the unborn child's spirit to a lonely afterlife. The *mizuko* ritual is meant to resolve that.

Through the *mizuko jizo* figure, the Japanese establish a connection between the unborn and the parents they might have known. Seeking the guardian's help for their unborn children, ministering to the needs of their *mizuko jizo* statues with food and clothing, naming their unborn children so their ancestors in the afterworld will recognize them when they come, sending their prayers, and buying them toys—in all these ways does this culture attest to the reality of, the potential for feeling and awareness of, and the worthiness of the unborn spirit. In all these ways does the culture look outside itself to its children after death, focusing on the children's well-being, their growth, and their eventual return.

Acknowledging the Unborn

Attributing that precious aspect that we call spirit to the unborn child allows it a worthiness we don't always give it in the West. And in the silence that we keep about our unborn children, we make a problem nearly unsolvable. It's just about impossible to heal from the loss of something that you must not admit is real.

What if our culture permitted the expression of love and of regret for the spirit that does not come to term or comes stillborn? Would Andrea's sorrow have been less if she had been allowed to bury her unborn child or bury a symbolic replica of it, or if she were a Karanga woman and could have sent the spirit of her unborn child off into the universe in a *gambe*-jar?

If we had a way to acknowledge our grief for those children who die before birth, then someone like Natalie might find it possible to face up to the reality of her loss, and her focus would be as much outside herself as inward. She would make sure there was no physical cause for her miscarriage, and then she would turn her attention to the unborn spirit that had touched her so briefly. She would wish it well on its journey; she might pray for its safety; she might take comfort in the idea of its return.

We put all sorts of conditions on our grief. Natalie required a full trimester of fetal development before she felt justified to mourn. Andrea couldn't bear to think of her baby as "real."

But, in fact, these women had carried something "real" inside, and both had lost a child that might have been. And these were most assuredly vital losses.

What I have learned from all this is that the unborn child is deserving of our grief, that its "might have been" needs the language to acknowledge it—through words or deeds or art or ritual—and that its loss requires, and sometimes demands, our purposeful healing action.

CHAPTER EIGHT

Can I Help My Child Where She's Gone?

Helping Rituals, Reasserting Our Power

The Need to Do Something

One of the great miseries that we go through when we lose the child we love is our feeling of powerlessness in the face of such a catastrophe. There is nothing we can do to change what is past, but "doing" is a solution to the desperate drive to have some effect on the present and ultimately on the future after our children die.

I believe that most of the people who have come to see me after the death of a child come because they feel they must do *something,* whether that is to try to learn why their child died, as it was for Sara's parents, Myra and Robert, or to make some positive gesture, as Andrea did by seeking to end her crying and by asking her priest to say a mass for her unborn child.

Usually the people who come to see me are looking for something to do that will help them feel better, something that can hasten their return to "normality." When Winnie came to see me all those years ago, she came to *do something* about her feeling of responsibility in her grandson's death. When Daniel grieved over losing Jesse, he threw himself almost compulsively into rebuilding the family's home—it was his way of *doing something* to distract himself from his sorrow. Natalie's global search for a biological explanation for her miscarriage may not have been absolutely reasonable, but it was another way of *doing*.

In order to facilitate our healing, we *do* other things in this culture after the death of our children. The first action is usually funeral arrangements. "Compared to what came after, it was the easiest part," one mother told me. "Contacting the mortuary, notifying family and friends, dealing with the cemetery, securing the church for the funeral, making sure there was food for everyone afterward—it gave me something to do at first. It kept me from falling into hell, where I went directly from the cemetery."

To avoid that hell, we make a Herculean effort. We return to the church or the temple. We throw ourselves back into our work. We begin seeing a therapist. We take a trip. We join groups like The Compassionate Friends, where we can find support.[1]

These are all positive actions. They may well be good things to do. They may very well help us and our recovery. But they don't do anything for the child we have lost.

In other cultures parents and other family members and friends of children who die believe they can do something, can take some action *on behalf of the deceased child*—and in addition to or as a by-product of doing something for their child, they also do something good for themselves.

Helping Rituals

Rituals are traditional, formal, or ceremonial acts or procedures. They are not just celebrations; they are not simply memorial events, although a ritual may occur at either of these. What defines ritual and distinguishes it from other big life events is that ritual can remove us for a little while from the everyday world to the world of the spirit, from the mundane world to the sacred one.

For many people in many places in the world, ritual is actually *part* of the everyday world. Throughout Japan, Jizo figures representing the ritual for the unborn are visible in private homes and public places. People in Bali eat and breathe ritual, rising early to set out offerings of food and flowers for their gods. Islam's day is built around ritual prayer.

In the West we treat rituals rather differently. They are special occasions; they are birthday celebrations, retirement parties, funerals, marriages, graduations; they are our rites of passage. Or they are customs, traditions in the making: we light candles with our evening meal and call it a ritual. We may enjoy our rituals, but they don't necessarily connect us with the world where spirit lives.

But in places where ritual is natural to the people, where it is steeped in the tradition of the people, where its power to move us from the mundane world to the world of spirit is well understood, it has great healing properties. And for families who have lost a child, rituals to help that child on her journey to the next world and, later, rituals that keep her happy in that world are the answer to "What can I do to help my child?"

True rituals are often very intricate affairs requiring extraordinary concentration. The mind does not wander; extraneous thoughts fall away. Sometimes the power of our concentration alone can transport us to where our children are, in that "virtual reality" of the imagination that the Spiritists describe. Sometimes, if our concentration is good enough, we may see evidence of our children's existence after death.

In the north of Japan, for instance, families of children who have died may attend one of twice-yearly rituals where blind mediums serve as living Jizos, guardians to the children crossing into the afterworld. The families line up along one side of a certain rock-strewn valley where the children will make their crossing. The mediums stand with the families and relate the children's progress. By concentrating very hard and watching very carefully, it is said that as the children step across the valley floor, their parents will see the rocks turn into eggshells.[2]

Funeral Rituals Among
the Hindu People

The Hindus say that no rituals are necessary after death for children who don't yet walk, for they are considered "divine souls," gods themselves, who ascend into the next world instantly and need no protection. For somewhat older children and for those past puberty who may have acquired karmic penalties, an elaborate cremation ritual assures the family that the child will enter the next world free of sin. The Mahapatra in Varanasi told me that these days children become worldly much earlier than previously, and now parents often do cremate the body of a child as young as five or seven years just to be sure any inadvertent sins are burned away.

Among the Hindu people I found the most intricate after-death rituals for children. Two struck me in particular. One is the *Dashgatra,* which is performed four days after the child's cremation. This ritual creates a "subtle body" out of rice for the child whose physical body has been consumed by cremation.

Ten mounds of cooked rice are patted into shape, each mound representing a different part of the body. Then water is poured over each mound of rice, beginning with the one that represents the head and concluding with the two that represent the feet. This watering symbolizes a cool bath to relieve the burning sensation caused by the cremation and to make up for the spirit's lost fluids. Milk is offered next, from a separate earthen vessel, because milk soothes the heat inside the body. At the end of the ritual, the "subtle body" is considered to be whole and hungry, and an eleventh offering of rice is made to satisfy the spirit's appetite.

The careful construction of a symbolic rice body is supposed to help the child and nourish him, but it also helps the parents visualize their child's body restored to wholeness. Participants chant in accompaniment with each poured "drink," and the family's undivided attention is

113

devoted to helping their child in this period after death. In this way, in the very early days of separation, they continue their connection with him. In this way they help him on his way to a better existence in a better place.

The *Dashgatra* ritual ends on the fifth day after death, when a Brahman child of the same age as the dead child is invited to the dead child's home and fed and given gifts of money, clothes, and utensils.

I have spoken with a mother whose son's body was never recovered from Vietnam. This young man's mother fears that his spirit wanders the earth, lost and alone. She is tortured by the fact that her child is not properly laid to rest. I wonder if her grieving would be any easier if she were a Hindu and a version of the *Dashgatra* ritual could be performed for her son, as if to restore his body. I wonder what power such an amended ritual might have for other families of children who are missing and presumed dead or for the parents of children whose bodies were badly damaged or unrecognizable in death.

This *Dashgatra* is a foreign concept, not in our language, not a ritual we are likely to perform, but is there something we could use instead to restore our child's body in our minds, in our imaginations? A photograph, perhaps, that we could speak to, that we could reassure. Or some representational object, like the *mizuko jizo* figure, or some other icon that we could lay to rest in place of our lost child.

The Hindus believe that the special suffering of children who die by violence or in a violent accident deserves special treatment in the next world. The *Narayan Bali* is a ritual only for children who die violently.

A Mahapatra conducts this ritual, chanting mantras to call each of seven Hindu gods to participate. Each god is represented by a metal image or statue. Each statue sits on one of seven pitchers. Each pitcher is covered with a cloth of a different color, and each color is specific to one of the seven gods whose spirits are in attendance. In the presence of this congregation of deities, a coconut is fed to a fire, symbolizing the child's head in a cremation ceremony.

As the fire transforms the coconut head, the god Vishnu is believed to step forward to "bond" with the spirit of the child. Vishnu's loving attention guarantees the child a blessed life after death, and the child's violent death is converted into a family's sacrifice to their god.

Imagine these kinds of elaborate, purposeful, detailed activities applied to the violent or accidental deaths of our own children to assure them the best possible future. How far they seem from Winnie's funeral for her grandson and his wife, at which she sat in a room full of many strangers and television cameras, searching herself for where she had failed them, believing that now they were beyond her help.

The Special Case of
a Twin Who Dies

When I learned about the special rituals performed throughout much of West Africa after the death of a twin, I was impressed once again by how many other cultures believe that we can help a child who has died. And I was once again aware of how the chaotic feelings that we carry inside after the death of a child can be eased by these special rituals, and how healing that can be. The rituals performed for twins in particular made me think of Daniel and Evelyn and their two surviving children—the whole family had suffered so much when Frankie's twin brother, Jesse, died at almost four years old.

The Yoruba of western Africa consider twins to be sacred children, spirits right here on earth, and they are treated with great love and tenderness. One tries never to offend a twin. Therefore, if one of a pair of twins dies, the other is not told about it right away, for it is believed that the shock could make the surviving twin die. Yoruba parents tell the surviving child that his brother has gone on a very long journey to the market in Lagos, the capital of Nigeria, far, far away, to buy clothes for himself and his sibling. Twins are almost always dressed up and dressed alike in a Yoruba family, and they usually love clothes. The white lie is told to soften the depression in the surviving twin.

Meanwhile, immediately upon the twin's death, two wooden dolls are carved that are replicas of each of the twin children. The dolls are called *omolangidi,* "the child who cannot talk." One of the dolls is buried with the child who died, to keep him company. Otherwise, it is thought, he might persuade his surviving twin to come with him on his journey—this is, after all, their first separation. For the same reason, all of the deceased twin's clothes are removed from the house so that his brother will not touch them and be spirited away.

During his brother's absence "at the market in Lagos," the living twin cares for his companion doll. The twin symbolically feeds his doll a bite of every different food he himself is served at mealtimes; he changes its clothes; he undresses it at night. Whenever the living child receives a new set of clothes, a duplicate set is provided for the *omolangidi.* When the doll does not go out strapped to its sibling's back like an infant, it occupies a privileged place in the inner room of the house, where it is idolized and "lives" until the twin it represents returns to the family.

If a living twin becomes ill, the dead one is also assumed to be ill, and parents will try to care for both, offering sacrifices and performing rituals for the dead child as well as for the living one.

The very next child born into the family is believed to be the twin returned and is accepted as such by everyone, including the original twin and the entire community. Raised this way, the new child is not confused about the fact that his twin brother or sister is a year or more older than he.

If time goes by and the living twin matures and wants to marry, and his brother has not been reincarnated into the family, the wooden doll is paired with a carved wooden wife so that the deceased twin doesn't become jealous.

The rituals regarding twin children who die are part of the fabric of life for the families of twins in this culture; they keep whole families occupied with acts that will help provide for the best possible afterlife for their children who have gone "to the market in Lagos."

Ritual Is an Antidote
to Powerlessness

Insofar as ritual gives us something to do, which we are desperate for in the early stages of grieving for a child we love, it keeps us active and alive. It becomes a way to say, "I am not a victim; I am not at the mercy of this terrible thing that has happened." When ritual delivers us to the other side, to touch the place where spirit lives, it imbues us with an energy that *empowers* us.

Daniel did not have any such reference or ritual to put against his feeling of powerlessness, and Frankie might have been mortified in our culture to carry a doll. But how fortunate are those cultures that incorporate such helping rituals as the Yoruba have for their twins, the Japanese have for their unborn, and the Hindus have for their children who die violently.

Although the rituals we have described here are elaborate, they need not be. The Baha'is read prayers for the departed soul's welfare in the next life and then enjoy a great after-death feast that will be repeated on the anniversary of the child's death in years to come. They say that such feasting in the dead child's name brings her great happiness in the afterworld.

It's even possible to ritually send a gift into the next world for the child you love. In Singapore, on a street of a hundred tiny shops, I found one in which cartons of gifts for the dead rose ceiling high. There was everything—shirts and pants, dresses, hats, coats, shoes, jewelry, cigarettes, wallets, telephones, clocks, cars, camping sets, dinnerware, silverware, radios, televisions, gold bars, silver bars, paper money—all carefully wrapped and all made of paper. For a child you could find clothes just her size, a doll, her favorite food, a little bicycle, books. You would take your gift to a crossroads and burn it. Once burned, you would have, in essence, mailed your gift.

I'm not recommending we rush over to Manhattan's 42nd Street or any other "Crossroads to the World" and burn an offering on behalf of our children who have died. The act wouldn't have the integrity of tradition, nor would it be authentic. But these rituals contain a certain wisdom that bears thinking about, and perhaps there is a way for us to translate them for our own lives—maybe through our churches and temples and communities and traditions that are authentic to us. Maybe then we can touch that place where the very highest power is to be had and where we can fill up for a little while with the strength we need to become whole human beings again.

CHAPTER NINE

Can My Child Hear Me?

Calling the Children

"I talk to her every day," Robert said to me about his daughter, Sara, who died in the skiing accident. Most of us continue to speak with our children after they're gone—we just don't admit it. We're sensitive to how it might strike others if they knew. But we do it anyway. Speaking to our children after death is all about focusing on them, directing our questions, our love, our grief outward, in their direction, instead of inward at ourselves. And it comes naturally to us. We have the language for this.

We speak to them in our minds, in our prayers, in our dreams and journals, and in unmailed letters, and when they answer us, we alone hear them in our heads and hearts.

But there are cultures in which communicating with children after they die need not be entirely private.

Heidi's Story

Heidi was a client of mine in 1973. She was a clinical psychologist and in her forties when she first came to me. She was plump and petite, with a beautiful speaking voice, and she spoke in full sentences even at the worst of times. Her middle son, Lawrence, had died by drowning two months earlier.

In the beginning of our work together, it was not uncommon for her to simply sit in the chair in my office and say very little. On more than a couple of occasions, she fell asleep. I remembered Viktor Frankl's book *Man's Search for Meaning,* about his time in Auschwitz, in which he said that he would never wake a bunkmate from a nightmare because he knew that whatever his neighbor was dreaming had to be better than the waking reality. I didn't wake Heidi until our hour together was up.

Her terrible exhaustion eventually lifted, and within a few months Heidi stayed awake for our full sessions. We worked together for four years. Now it is sixteen years later, and I asked her to speak with me for this book about her experience after Lawrence died. I've transcribed her story with only the most minor editorial changes:

It was the day after Christmas, in Maine, on the Atlantic coast. I was told by the local sheriff that he was missing, probably drowned. But there was no place in my mind that opened to the fact that my son was not alive. I felt that he was missing, but only missing, and I prayed for him, which is not something I do. And I kept a vigil, sort of calling to him, hoping for him.

I can't remember how it was that the next day at around noon Lawrence's father and I went to the place they said he might be found if he had been swept away as they suspected. It was a very beautiful place actually. We passed Lawrence's shoes on the way— where he had taken them off before climbing down a very steep path to the ocean. And as we stood there, we saw his body wash up onto the beach. And he was naked.

It was quite an amazing experience. To say that I was stunned and shocked doesn't do justice to the experience. It was so totally different from anything I had ever known before. I never had thought about having a child die, as lots of women fear. I felt as if my feet were not touching the ground, that I was kind of lifted up and moved through space in some way that was indescribable.

Heidi received hundreds of letters, notes of condolence, full of comforting thoughts and love and support, "but also notes from friends, colleagues, peers who were more into the esoteric, who wrote about the meaning of a child dying. About Lawrence's need to be with God, about his spirit. Part of me believed, but part of me was enraged. How dare anybody presume to tell me there was any good reason for his death. But there were other moments when they comforted me."

A year after her son's death, Heidi and her husband traveled to Europe, and while she was there, "on a whim, really, because one of my friends had mentioned it to me," she visited the British College of Psychical Research in London for a consultation.

All I said was that I had lost a child, and told the woman that I wanted her to make contact with him. I can't remember the content of the reading exactly, but she had these physical details that just blew me away. About his shoes, for instance. That he had taken them off and where he had left them. Things that she had no way of knowing. She said she was making direct contact with him. He asked for his father by name, which I hadn't told her.

And she gave me many messages. She told me that he was fine, which was reassuring to me. That he was with his grandparents. And she said that he would always be with me. That he would be with me when I was working, that he would be with me when I was listening to music, that he would never leave me again. I have four living children. I still had to anticipate their going off to college, getting married, leaving home, but these were things that would never happen with Lawrence.

"It felt as if I were talking to him with this woman, although I wasn't sure I could believe it," Heidi said. But her sorrow shifted perceptibly afterward. She told me that she had felt cold until then, physically and emotionally. She had carried an extra sweater or shawl since the winter Lawrence died. She had found it hard to laugh. But that day she began to thaw. The reassurance Heidi gained from her psychic consultation was as profound as that gained when a physician friend explained Lawrence's autopsy report, letting her know that his death had very likely been a quick one, that he probably hadn't experienced even a second of terror.

Accessing and sharing this kind of information—from the medical to the metaphysical—is a way to expand our language on the subject of child death. The more we communicate with our child even after he is gone and with the professionals who can satisfy our need to understand the physical aspects of his death and with one another in developing an atmosphere in which healing is easier than now, the bigger the language grows. And the bigger the language, the more possible it becomes to answer our most urgent questions after our child's death.

Ways We Communicate with Our Children After Their Deaths

What was most interesting to me in Heidi's account were the many ways in which she was able to "communicate" with Lawrence after death. On the first night when he was missing, she says she felt as if she were "calling" him. She also told me that for weeks after he died, they "had talks every day. I felt like I was sort of helping him make an adjustment to this place he was going to and he was informing me where he was." By going further and consulting the psychic, Heidi managed to receive "messages" from him. These "communications" seemed perfectly natural. "It was *strange,*" she said, "but it didn't feel unnatural." In many other cultures that I have studied, it doesn't even qualify as strange to continue to engage in a dialog with the spirit that still exists after a loved one dies.

The Spiritists say that communication is never interrupted, only modified. As one thinks, so one communicates. Spiritists understand that the human mind is both a powerful transmitter and receiver. And although we're used to using our physical senses for communication, especially hearing, vocalizing, and seeing, the Spiritists say that in the spirit world, communication is telepathic. And it's not all that easy to achieve. Our senior researcher explains:

> Everyone can send messages across space, but communication will take place only if the receiver is ready and sensitive enough. Very much like telecommunications on earth, the signal must be sufficiently powerful and in the correct frequency of the receiver. . . . Prayer and meditation are two methods of going from medium- to short-wave reception, raising our own frequency in order to receive a higher order of vibrations.
>
> The process is somewhat complex and may be out of reach for the majority of spirits of average development. The process is several times harder for a child, particularly for a child who is only recently separated. At times, when it is necessary for a child to communicate with parents, mentors of the child [in the afterworld] lend their help.

In Bali, in order to talk to their children after death, it is common for parents to visit a Balian, a Balinese shaman and healer who is able to incorporate a child's spirit. Our senior researcher in Indonesia reports:

> The activity is called *maluasang*. The Balian will go into a trance state and contact the spirit. The spirit of the child will enter the Balian's body. As soon as the Balian starts speaking in the voice of

the child, the parents can talk to the child. I have observed touching scenes in which mothers fainted and fathers with tears in their eyes recognized the voice of their child. Sometimes family members are so overwhelmed by the situation that they fall into a trance themselves. Questions like "Why did you die?" "Where are you living now?" are asked by the parents and answered by the spirit of the child. I noticed great relief and satisfaction in the family after such a session.

Remember the Yakurr in Nigeria, whose deceased children listen intently to their commemoration at burial to decide where to return? When I asked our senior researcher for the Yakurr about ways they communicate with their children beyond the burial ritual, he told me this personal story:

A cousin of mine, Alice, gave birth to eleven children. Nine survived until last year, when one of her sons died suddenly at the age of ten. I was at home at the time the boy died. For months after his death, she continued to see him in her dreams and he seemed perfectly the same as when he was alive, doing the same things that he used to do when he was alive. The dreams were so real indeed that she said she discussed with him the "rumor" of his death, and he was able to confirm to her that he was still alive and well. She said that she felt such relief both in the dream and after she woke up from her sleep.

After death a child continues to live with his family in a different form, so much so that some Yakurr mothers continue to leave food outside the house for their dead child. My cousin may have felt a sense of relief because her dream confirmed for her the continued existence of her son and his continued participation in the daily activities of the family. She suffered a loss, but it was limited in this way.

Deceased children appear frequently in the dreams of the ones who love them, and for many this is proof that their children still exist in another world. Among the people of the Nembe region, in the Niger Delta of Nigeria, it is said that children often appear in the dreams of women, running after them. If the adult dreamer is caught, the dream child will return to this life in her.

Calling the Children

Over the years, of the many parents who have spoken to me about talking to their children after death, some have been deeply embarrassed by it; some have taken it as a sign of neurosis or obsession; and some, like Heidi, have been totally unashamed and completely matter-of-fact. Most have taken invaluable comfort in it.

Of course, I only learn about this kind of communication secondhand. The talks between a mother and a dead child or between siblings, one alive, one not, are very intimate communions. But in 1996, when I traveled in Brazil, a country where the spirit world lives very close to us, I was introduced to an Umbanda priestess whose communication with dead children was a very public affair.

Umbanda is a major spiritual-religious system with millions of followers, one of the most widespread and popular in Brazil. It contains elements of the African-based Candomblé system, which arrived on the continent during the seventeenth century on slave ships; aspects of even older Brazilian Indian beliefs; some Catholicism; and parts of Allan Kardec's Spiritist thinking, including the possibility of communicating with the spirit world. Umbanda is an amalgam of philosophy and religion and culture, a lot like Brazil itself.

My partner in research, Edmundo Barbosa, had heard about a *Mi de Santo*, Mother of the Saints, who conducted an Umbanda ritual in which she "called" the spirits of dead children. We didn't know a whole lot more than that and the woman's name, which was Baby.

We found her not far from where Edmundo lives in São Paulo and arranged an introduction through a mutual friend. Baby was an articulate Umbandista of the highest rank and absolutely down to earth. She understood English and spoke it a little bit, but Edmundo translated for us in his usual seamless style so that the experience for me was of speaking directly with her.

Handsome, humorous, tall, blonde, in her forties, with that very unlikely name, she smoked my cigarettes and listened solemnly to my interest in the ongoing relationship that might exist between children who have died and their family and friends.

On Tuesday, she told us, she would be conducting her usual Umbanda ritual for the general public at the Temple Guaraci, where she presided then, and if we would like to stay afterward, she would extend the ritual to "call the children" and I could ask them my questions. Calling the children must be done between 9:00 and 10:00 P.M., she explained, and only on specific days, when they are receptive.

In the Temple

Edmundo and I arrived at the temple at around 7:00 P.M. The sound of drums spilled out of open doors and windows, and over that we could hear the chanting and singing of the initiates and strong, rhythmic clapping.

Initiates among the Umbanda are an elite group of men and women who have gone through powerful rituals of indoctrination and many years of education and practice for their special role in the community. Initiates here provide bodies for ancestor spirits to communicate with living people on all manner of subjects, from the material to the spiritual.

The temple's main room was brightly lit, with an inner sanctum separated by a low railing behind which there were chairs for the congregation and visitors. Inside the railing, in an area 20 by 80 feet, a raised altar took up the back wall. The drummers sat to the left of the altar, and the initiates milled in front of it. They were all dressed in brilliant white, the women in voluminous lace skirts with puffed sleeves and lots of petticoats. Baby was in the very center of it all. There was a lot of movement, a lot of undulating white, and layer upon layer of lace inside the railing.

Outside the railing the scene was a lot like a company picnic without the barbecue. Kids were running around, and people were sitting or standing in groups of three or four or more, some keeping the rhythm of the drums, clapping, some just watching. There didn't appear to be any church service about to begin; there were no prayer books. It looked like a warm, upbeat community get-together.

Very slowly, over a period of a half hour or so, the atmosphere in the room began to change. The drums became louder and faster, and a few of the initiates began dancing. Soon they were twirling, and the women's petticoats were contributing their own whooshing music. The three drummers were beating a much faster, insistent rhythm that they had been building up to all along. Without my having noticed it happen, suddenly the place was absolutely vibrating.

Edmundo told me to watch Baby as she exchanged the bright turquoise head scarf she had been wearing for a magnificent two-foot-tall, feathered Indian headpiece. Then she lit a cigar! Then all the initiates, men and women, lit cigars! This signaled that the African-slave and Indian ancestors had entered the bodies of the initiates. (The ancients are said to enjoy a good cigar, and cigar smoke is supposed to dispel evil spirits.)

As the initiates received their spirits, the dancing ceased and the drums steadied, although the feeling of a highly charged atmosphere remained. Now people ventured inside the railings to ask for advice.

Some just asked for a blessing. Other people provided earnest explanations and descriptions, and the initiates listened carefully, puffing thoughtfully and then responding with the wisdom of the long-dead spirits speaking through them.

It was an active, almost frenetic scene—clusters of three or more people in animated conversation, an initiate occasionally breaking into dance or twirling in place, a woman crying and nodding at what the initiate-spirit was saying to her, clouds of cigar smoke, laughter, children running, playing, squealing, and drums drumming.

Edmundo and I stood at the railing. Suddenly he grabbed my shoulder. "Now!" he said, picking up on a subtle change in the drums. "She's calling them—move!" And he shoved me forward, dragging the tape recorder, pushing past the people in front of me and propelling us into the center of the room, where pandemonium reigned.

Baby had signaled the drummers; in fact, it was they who called the children. The drum rhythm had completely changed, and there, all around me, crawling, sprawling, wailing, giggling, and drooling on the floor, were a dozen initiates who until minutes ago had contained the spirits of the ancestors but now were inhabited by the spirits of eight or so children of various ages.

The other initiates stood by these child spirits, watching over them, making sure they weren't stepped on, because in a minute everyone in the room had moved in to play with them. Many had brought wrapped candy; many had toys. Even I had come prepared, with pockets full of candy and balloons and a miniature plastic dinosaur.

What I hadn't been prepared for was the chaos. I didn't know exactly what to do. In the turmoil my attention was caught by an initiate who sat a little apart, rocking back and forth, reminiscent of the autistic children I had once worked with, but I hardly had time to register this when Edmundo whispered, "Here they come!"

Two initiates were approaching. They moved just like very young children, crawling so fast they nearly tumbled over each other. They sounded like children, acted like children, but they had borrowed the bodies of adults. When I closed my eyes, I believed I was in a room full of children. When I opened my eyes, I could have believed it was some kind of asylum. I got down on the floor with them.

The two "children" were focused on the tape recorder. One held a clear plastic purse in which she had been collecting candy. She wore big pink plastic-framed glasses and a rainbow-colored ribbon in her hair. I said, "Hi, who are you?" but she ignored me until Edmundo translated. Then she answered proudly, "Aninha," Little Anna, and she was seven years old.

The other "child" watched us. I took the dinosaur out of my pocket and placed it in the bed of a toy truck he was carrying. His name was Little Joseph. He was four.

Although many people remained outside the railing, many more, children and adults, had come inside to play with the adult-children now among us. The place buzzed with chatter and laughter, everybody animated, happy; the drums and the atmosphere were still keeping everyone energized.

A half hour must have passed this way, but the questions I managed to ask elicited blank stares or non sequiturs. "Little Joseph," I said, "Do you know *why* you died?" At Edmundo's translation, Little Joseph looked at me as if I were a little dim and said, "I'm not dead!"

When I asked Aninha if her family was here tonight, Edmundo translated her reply: "I would like to have the pink balloon." When I asked, "Where do you come from?" she said she would also have the white balloon.

At the end, Baby strode in among all the children to say it was time to leave. Aninha kissed me very lightly, very sweetly, a little peppermint-stickily, once on the cheek—usually Brazilians kiss both cheeks—and Little Joseph also exchanged a single kiss with me. And then they were gone, the crowd sort of swallowing them up.

Meeting the Initiates

We had arranged to meet the initiates who had incorporated Aninha and Little Joseph after the ritual. At around 10:30 P.M., Edmundo and I were waiting in a comfortable room furnished with a sofa and soft chairs upstairs in the temple when a man and woman entered. Edmundo rose and went to greet them. Friends of his, I thought, but then I heard him say, laughingly, how much we enjoyed playing with them.

I couldn't believe it. This couple looked nothing like the two we had spent a half hour with only minutes before! Although I had stared into their eyes, kissed their cheeks, and held their hands, I would never have recognized them. Now they wore street clothes, no longer their white ceremonial dress, no rainbow ribbon, no pink glasses, no plastic purse. But that didn't seem enough reason for this astonishing change. Both seemed in their thirties. Both were a little shy.

They introduced themselves as Belinda and Ulysses. She was a large-breasted woman, very sensuous looking, with a beautiful smile. Ulysses was a small, slender man with a mustache, which I hadn't even noticed on Little Joseph. We exchanged kisses, this time in the Brazilian way. I said I didn't recognize them, and they both laughed. Then I asked permission to ask some questions. They were happy to answer, they said.

"When did Aninha die?" I asked Belinda. At the age of seven. How did she die? She was hit by a train. She lost both her legs in the accident, which is why she doesn't stand but only crawls, Belinda said. I hadn't realized that she didn't walk. As strange as the experience had been, I was now as amazed at what had gone by unnoticed.

When she first incorporated Aninha, nearly five years ago, she was a sad child, Belinda told me. So Belinda had brought her presents—dolls and ribbons, the plastic purse, the pink glasses—and over time Aninha had become the cheerful little girl she was today.

"Do you know *why* Aninha died as a child? I asked. She did not. "Do you know who her parents were?" She didn't know. "Can you tell me about where Aninha lives now? She could not, Belinda said apologetically.

But Ulysses was able to say something about Little Joseph's after-death experience. Little Joseph had been the only child of an older couple who had despaired of ever having a child. Little Joseph was their gift, Ulysses said, but he drowned in a waterfall. Afterward he awoke by a river in Aruanda (heaven) in the arms of a black man, once a slave named Pi Ja Cato. Ulysses also incorporated Pi Ja Cato's spirit.

Both Ulysses and Belinda seemed perfectly normal, but still I wondered about their mental health. I asked Belinda if she had been a happy child, and she answered yes. She had been raised in Rio in a close family, all of whom were members of temple, by the way, and all of whom had been present tonight. Belinda had been a schoolteacher but was not teaching currently. She could not have children herself because of some medical condition.

"Do you like Aninha?" I asked. "Oh, yes," she said. "I like Aninha very much."

As for Ulysses, he was a policeman in real life. His wife had gotten him involved in the temple. They had three children. "Have your children met Little Joseph?" I asked.

"Yes, of course," he said. When his sons were younger, they used to come every Friday night, the usual night for the children to manifest, especially to play with Little Joseph. Sometimes Little Joseph was able to explain things to them that their father, Ulysses, couldn't. For instance, Little Joseph had taught both boys how to tie their shoes.

I was back in a familiar other reality, that of therapist and researcher trying to ask the right questions of myself as well as my subjects. As reasonable as both these well-spoken people were, my Western brain tried to find some explanation for why they believed they could incorporate the spirits of dead children. Something to do with the inner child? I wondered.

But I have been with the inner children of clients in therapeutic sessions. I have spoken to these inner children and they have spoken to me, and although our dialogues have been animated and frequently amazingly informative, the experience has never been as authentic, consistent, and *sincere* as this evening's. I have also sat on the floor and played with some seriously regressed people in Bellevue Psychiatric Hospital in New York—also something I'll never forget, but nothing like this.

Belinda seemed to read my thoughts. "Some of the children are dead and some are not," she volunteered.

> Some may well be past-life recalls. Certainly what we are involved with taps into the inner child in some way, but more we are engaging with other dimensions of reality that are present all the time but not so easy to touch.
>
> We want to bring the joy of the child, the imagination, curiosity, and openness back into mankind. It has been lost somewhere. These children that we bring are for that—to heal the wound of not having a child in us as a people.

It was not a seven-year-old speaking. Nor a multiple personality nor an exhibitionist nor a woman compensating for having no children of her own.

I felt myself blush. I was wondering about her sanity, and she not only read my mind but gave me two possibilities to choose from. These incorporations could go either way: They might be a conduit for actual child spirits or a means for restoring and maintaining the greater spirit of the child in one's community, which struck me as psychologically a very interesting idea.

What if Belinda were right? What if part of our difficulty healing from the loss of a child had to do with our difficulty in maintaining our culture's child spirit or our own? Maybe this is part of the reason that we die a little ourselves when our children die. They have provided the child spirit incarnate; now that they are gone, we may feel as if all innocence is gone from our life as well, and all sweetness. And we may be right.

And what if we actually can communicate with our dead children? What if that were true? Then when we say, "I love you" and "I miss you," they are reassured. Then when we confide in them, they feel our confidence. Then how much less lost to us they are! Even if it *is* one-sided, even if we cannot hear them answer but only *feel* them answer, even if we do not feel them but only *imagine* them receiving what we say or hope for them, how much less lost to us they are.

Communication Is an Antidote
to Our Lack of Language

As part of our intentional building of a language that can help us talk about the death of our children, that might open us to comfort when they have left our world, that *will* help us heal, I suggest that we "out" the phenomenon of after-death communication. Everybody does it, so why not admit it?

Why is it shameful, anyway? Saying "I dreamed about Jesse last night" brings Jesse back into the household while we share the dream. Saying "I saw a young couple today who reminded me of Seth and Jill" allows those spirits to enter and inhabit our airwaves for at least as long as they are in our thoughts and conversation.

When they come, however they come, these visitations are infusions of spiritual energy in our everyday lives. They aren't spooky. They're not weird. They're definitely not unusual. If nothing more, we could look at the dreams, the remembrances, the fleeting thoughts, the imagined conversations, and the daydreams as blessings.

PART THREE

Language When a Child Dies

We have taken a step by beginning to speak about one of the most terrible losses in the world. We have approached the subject with some caution, trying to understand how our agony is exacerbated by our own cultural traditions, imagining the ways that other traditions perceive of and treat the same loss.

Like a jigsaw puzzle, every individual piece of information we have related here, from Native American customs to those in Africa, Brazil, Japan, Indonesia, and elsewhere, gives us a hint of the whole picture. Together, all these pieces—the idea of destiny, the concept of time and life as a continuum, the possibility of fuller communication than we normally know, the rituals for helping and healing—may tell us some truth about our children's future after death and, maybe as important, some truth about our own survival after.

Ultimately, though, our recovery is not likely to be earned at the expense of our own culture and traditions. The Yoruba diviner will probably not be able to help us avoid another miscarriage. We will not call upon the guardian Jizo to accompany our child across the river to the next world, as the Japanese do, or fabricate a "subtle body" for her after cremation, as the Hindus do, to ensure for her the best possible future. But together the force of these other world views regarding the life after death of a child might push open a door for us in how we think about our own children after death. And from this entranceway it may be possible to return to the world as whole people again.

How we come back, and who we are when we return, is the subject of Part Three of this book.

CHAPTER TEN

The Other Side of Our Mirror of God

Everything is Different, Inside and Out

It is common for the members of a grieving family to feel as if they've been lifted out of the world they know and dropped into another reality. They continue to exist—they walk around, perform various tasks—the environment looks just as it did, but it is not the same. Something is terribly different, and the difference is more than just the absence of the child who has died.

Myra and Robert described the phenomenon as having walked through Alice's looking glass. My metaphor is the mirror of God. This is indeed what life is like after the mirror in which we see ourselves as God is shattered. A different world, a different landscape stretches to the horizon for eternity on the other side of the glass. Not only is there limited language here with which we might begin to define our new circumstances and condition, but our old vocabulary has lost a great deal of its meaning. Words like *together* and *forever* and *mine* and *belief* are not to be entirely trusted anymore.

Who we are inside is different and how we relate to the world is different after the loss of a child. How we see and experience things is quite, quite different. Much of what we believed was true is no longer true. We feel unsafe. We feel our children are not safe. Now we feel as if we have no power to protect ourselves or them. It is not always a wonderful world after all.

Who we are outside is different too. How we see ourselves and how others see and define us have changed radically. Barbara is no longer the mother of Zach, the A student; Daniel is not just the successful architect, nor Winnie the matriarch of a large devout family. Now Barbara is the one whose son died in a car wreck; Daniel has become that talented man who was never the same after one of his twin boys died; and Winnie is the lady whose grandson was murdered so horribly. And this is who they will always be, in addition to whatever else they are or become after their children have died.

Our World and Our World View
Have Changed

Not only have we changed inside and out, but the world around us has changed as well. The world we occupied in relation to our child—a world full of its own drama as the child grew, a world full of emotion and potential—dissolves abruptly. If we even try to visit it, we find ourselves floating on an ocean of chaos and despair. Even our everyday world, the mundane world of grocery shopping and dental appointments, and any future world of plans or dreams may seem meaningless and even repugnant.

In addition to everything else, when we lose a beloved child, we also lose our world view, how we understand life in general and our lives in particular. The ordered universe in which we trusted has turned to chaos. Even our community of friends and family becomes estranged when our child dies, because speaking of this kind of tragedy is so difficult and because we are not the person we used to be, not anyone like the one they once knew and could relate to and loved. We don't even speak the same language anymore.

We may never have realized how many worlds we inhabit at one time. Now our inner world, the outer world, the world in which our child used to live, the world in which she no longer lives, the world of pain, the world of dreams, and our place in the world, all have shifted on their axis.

As we reenter the world and life around us, we are strangers, even to ourselves. No wonder it is so difficult to approach us. No wonder it is so difficult to reach out.

Daniel and Evelyn, Continued

Time passes. Many years go by, and we are only just "recovering" from the shock. Some of my colleagues say it takes five to seven years to really return to life from the death of a child. Regardless of the length of time it takes, there is much to endure, including the seven guilts we associate with child death, the tendency to freeze the child, the challenges to our faith and our relationships. Only after dealing in some way with these issues may we begin accepting the possibility of some kind of long-term recovery, because we have finally come to understand that nothing will ever be as it was before, not even us. We know now that we are members for life of a society we didn't even realize existed and never asked to join.

This understanding is a powerful aftershock that can be especially wrenching to our relationships. We choose a partner and set out on a path together with certain shared expectations about life. With the death of our child, our destination is uncertain. Those expectations may appear to be absurd vanities, and our path may seem ruined by potholes and detours that fork off in unexpected directions.

Such was the case for Daniel and Evelyn. After six years he had not resolved what felt like his "comeuppance," in his words—a kind of mortification that he wasn't the man he had thought he was. In fact, Daniel *wasn't* the man he had been while Jesse lived. That Daniel had been optimistic, enthusiastic, extroverted, even a little brash. This Daniel was pessimistic, disappointed, and withdrawn. Their sex life suffered. Daniel came to therapy with Evelyn a couple of times but said that he found talking about their problems only made him feel worse. Nor was he interested in trying antidepressants or a support group.

Evelyn worked hard to keep him buoyant, as their daughter Jennifer did, but it wasn't easy, and one day Evelyn awoke with a new thought. "I realized suddenly that we hadn't really lost Jesse," she told me. "Jesse was in our hearts. We could even 'see' Jesse just by looking at Frank. But Daniel really was gone from us."

Approaching him to discuss a separation, Evelyn drew on a well of courage she had never known she possessed. There was no animosity between them. "He said he knew that this was no kind of life for the children or me," she told me. "But he said he didn't have the strength to make a change or even suggest one. He told me he was proud of me. He told me, believe it or not, he was grateful."

Evelyn had changed from a woman who could not speak at her son's memorial to one with the words that freed her to enter life again. Somehow she had found the doorway back.

Myra and Robert, Continued

Sara's parents were lucky to land together in their new world. More couples than not are torn apart after a child's death in the family. But Myra and Robert very much experienced the same things and by leaning together kept themselves upright. At the same time, as is the case for many other families after the death of a child, they both experienced a loss of faith. What Robert had feared, that he would despise God, looked like an inevitable consequence of Sara's death.

Life in this strange, familiar land we return to, usually many years after our child has died, seems like a series of robberies as we discover aspects of our old life that are missing now. Our innocence is gone, and so is our faith in the future. Sometimes the love that bound us to our husband or wife disappears in the depths of our unhappiness.

This was not the case for Myra and Robert; if anything, they became more devoted to each other. But for them, faith in God became one of those missing parts. Ultimately, they stopped going to their temple, stopped keeping the Jewish holidays, and for a time renounced a religious life altogether.

This need not always be the case. The world we inhabit after our children die can include God. We can believe again, though *what* we believe and *how* we believe will surely be different than before.

Renewing Faith

While some surveys show that as many as 50 to 70 percent of couples split up after the death of a child, a psychological study of childbearing loss by R. J. Knapp finds "a high incidence in the change of the survivor's religious orientation in a positive direction. Over 70 percent reported a renewed or intensified belief in a spiritual dimension. Thus, a significant number of parents reported that they were no longer afraid of death itself and were more able to relish life and its offerings."[1]

How do we get from that place of distrust or rejection of God to a place of peace and love of God? When our child dies and our mirror of God shatters, we no longer see ourselves as God, and we no longer see God as we wish Him to be. And then we have two choices. We can reject God. This is a harsh path because when we do so, we also reject the possibility of miracles and the mysterious, of spirit life and spirituality—elements that add the fabulous to mundane existence and make life so much richer. We would surely be giving up the possibility of connecting with the spirit of our child by denying these spiritual things. We might even be denying an aspect of ourselves.

Or we can accept God as something far more complex than we knew, not all love and sunshine but, like nature, part thunder and fury and capable of great destruction. Religious scholar David R. Blumenthal writes, "We cannot understand God (or ourselves) if we censor out what we do not like, or what we would like not to see."[2] But if we look without censorship, a new acceptance of God and a new relationship with God are possible.

And just as it's possible to reform our spiritual lives after the death of our children, other aspects of our lives can be restored too. I don't mean that we must settle for a life that's second best or make-do. I think we can become whole people again and of the world again. And I think our return must begin with the language.

An Old Word for Who We Are
After Our Child Has Died

In our search for a meaningful vocabulary for the experience of child loss, we need words that will contain the pain and isolation and chaos and the spiritual upheaval of all that has transpired. We need words that symbolize both suffering and healing, that evoke honor and suggest experience, new strength, and deeper vision—because all these are true after the death of a child.

I would like to propose that those of us who have lost a child and been through the horror of it—dealt with the guilts and the sorrow, had the scales removed from our eyes, and are still standing—I would like to say that we are, in the strictest sense of the word, initiates. I would like to suggest that we might well think of ourselves, and that the world might also think of us, as initiates.

We know the word in this culture in terms of honor societies, fraternities and sororities, and Masonic orders, but in the context of a child's death, I mean something quite different. Consider the word *initiation* as the renowned anthropologist and expert in ritual and initiation, Mircea Eliade, defines it: "Initiation is the equivalent to a basic change in [the] existential condition; the novice emerges from his ordeal endowed with a totally different being from that which he possessed before his initiation; he has become *another.*"[3]

I think of the Umbanda initiates who must begin as novices, who endure a several-years-long period of ritual and education, and who emerge endowed with the ability to speak in the tongues of their revered ancestors.

How we see, what we know, how we understand life are entirely different after initiation. How we are seen, how we are understood, and who we are in our community are also entirely different. It is just as Eliade says, "a basic change in the existential condition." Once initiated, we are no longer innocents, and everyone knows it.

When we are initiated, Eliade says, we receive "a crucial revelation of the world and of life." Our consciousness is changed and changed forever. And Eliade goes a step further to say that "before initiation, one does not share fully in the human condition."[4]

Only after initiation are we fully human. What does this mean? I think being *fully* human means becoming a whole human, and being whole is another way of speaking about healing and about completion.

I think being *fully* human also means having the greatest possible access to all of one's humanity—including qualities that may have been only partially available to us before or that we didn't even know we possessed at all.

Perhaps most profoundly, I believe that being fully human can finally deliver us to a place from which we can admit that we are *only* human.

To be *only* human. Think of it.

To be only human means that we are no longer pretenders to God. And this, finally, is what may allow us to return to God, though as in everything else after the death of our child, not in the same way as before.

CHAPTER ELEVEN

Initiation

In the 1980s on an island off the coast of Brazil, I attended the initiation of a young man into the ranks of Egun-gun, a special cult within what is the oldest and purest of the Afro-Brazilian traditions, called Candomblé.

I hadn't intended to go to an initiation. I didn't even think it was possible for an outsider to attend. I had heard that these initiations were terribly strange, even frightening for someone outside the culture. As part of the research for my first book, I was there to see *another* very rare ritual—the Return of the Dead—at which the community's deceased ancestors return.[1] This was difficult enough to manage an invitation to. It took a full two years from the time we were invited until the time we were allowed to attend.

The inauguration of the new initiate immediately preceded the ritual I had come to see. No one had mentioned that this would be happening. I was unprepared in every way for what I would witness.

It took place on the night we arrived. It was held inside a temple that was actually a large room with an earth floor, windows shuttered on all sides, an open bathroom in the back, and a simple altar in the front. All the members of the initiate's community were there, from babes in arms to the very elderly. People had brought blankets and spread them out on the floor and were picnicking on sweets and crackers. Neighbors were talking; teenagers were flirting; there were drums beating and cowbells ringing. As in the Umbanda ritual I had witnessed in São Paulo, everything leading up to it was as normal and unhurried and pleasant as could be.

And then suddenly, with no warning, the sound of the drums exploded and a young man in his twenties was literally flung into the temple room, pushed, shoved, hurled forward through all of us gathered there. Three men propelled him up to the front of the temple, where he was held to his knees. The sight of him as he hurtled past stunned me: he was naked except for a loincloth; his blue-black skin gleamed with sweat; and a grimace of terror stretched across his face.

Then the chief of Egun, a powerful-looking man, strode to the front of the temple. With one arm he swung two roosters by their necks. A goat on a tether was lashed to his other arm.

The drums were wild; the bells clanged; the goat bleated pitifully. As soon as he got to the altar, the chief slit the goat's throat. Two men lifted it upside down, and its blood poured into a bucket. The drums beat even faster. I'm pretty sure that without those drums insisting that I remain conscious, I would certainly have fainted.

The young man crouched, holding himself, trembling on the floor. Then in one horrifying moment the bucketful of goat's blood was flung at him and he was drenched in it. It slid down his face, still contorted as if in terrible pain. It slid down his chest; it slid over his thighs. And then somebody hoisted another bucket, this one full of feathers, and now the young man was covered in blood and feathers, and he was wracked with sobs.

The drums slowed and quieted, but they never stopped. A man knelt next to the new initiate, helped him to his feet, and led him out of the temple. He was taken to a house a short distance from the temple. There he would bathe; he might sleep; he would be offered food. He would remain apart from people for a while.

I don't know how the aftermath went exactly. In other Candomblé initiations the mandatory period of isolation may be in silence and last for a period of seventeen to thirty days. During this time initiates are led back and forth to the temple to make ritual offerings to strengthen the connection between themselves and the spirit forces with which they will become intimately associated in their new lives.[2] As in all rituals of initiation, when the initiate rejoins the community, he is someone quite different from who he was before, and he has gained the respect of every member of his society.

Watching the event had a profound effect on me. It has stayed vividly in my mind for more than ten years. It led me to books I never would have picked up otherwise; it inspired me to learn a great deal more about different kinds of initiation.

Two years after that spectacular night, on another trip of investigation to the same small island, I was introduced to the man I had seen initiated. His name was Sergio. He was warm and polite. He was also very handsome, but I remembered clearly the horror that had stretched his features into quite another face.

He was dressed in white on this occasion, in preparation for another ritual. He seemed much taller and more substantial than the wiry youth I remembered. I told him that I had been at his initiation, and he smiled. I asked him if it was as terrible as it had seemed to me, and he nodded affirmatively, still with a warm smile.

I asked him if he would choose to do it again. He corrected me gently: "I didn't choose to be initiated," he said. "It was decided for me." He had inherited the privilege of initiation from his father's family.

"Did the experience change you?" I asked.

"I am full in a way I was not before," he said.

Eight Dominant Themes
of Initiation

When I began working on this book and began to look at the experience of losing a child as a form of initiation, those memories of Sergio's experience and of subsequent other initiations I have attended affirmed the direction in which I was thinking. Although it may seem a stretch to compare what Sergio went through to what happens to us when our children die, walk a little way down this path with me. Let's open our imaginations to this possibility, as we have with the customs of other cultures in Part Two of this book.

The death of our child does not constitute initiation all by itself. But if we take the whole experience, from the moment of the death, through the shock of having lost the child, past the jumble of funeral arrangements, across the long years of guilt and rage and despair and loneliness and emptiness, and finally to the beginning of acceptance and the gradual reentry into life—a different life, with different expectations—all this could be called initiation.

"From a certain [structural] point of view," Mircea Eliade writes, "initiations are much alike." He refers to the following themes that are present in most initiations, whether they are into adulthood or secret societies or a mystical vocation. See how these same motifs speak with startling accuracy about our experience when we lose a child we love: (1) Initiation may be voluntary or not. (2) Initiation must be experienced "in person"; that is, we can't be initiated by reading about it or filling out an application and being chosen. We have to go *through* it; it has to *happen* to us. (3) Initiation requires witnesses. (4) Initiation includes chaos. (5) Initiation requires courage. (6) Initiation requires blood sacrifice. (7) Initiation requires a period of isolation. (8) Initiation includes the death of an aspect of oneself.[3]

Initiation may or may not be voluntary. Initiation is often chosen, but it is also true that we may be chosen for it. Certainly no one volunteers for initiation by means of the death of a child.

Sergio had not volunteered, he said, and I thought back to his grimace of terror, as if he were being torn apart inside. I think of the faces of my clients—how Barbara must have looked when she arrived out of breath and terrified at the hospital emergency room where Zach was pronounced dead, and how the agony was etched across Daniel's face when he spoke of losing Jesse.

Initiation is something you go through. Like all profound, life-altering experiences, initiation is not something we can truly understand secondhand. The description of Sergio's initiation may be startling, and I can attest that seeing it close up was horrifying, but neither of these responses or reactions can touch the effect of the experience on Sergio.

I remember Heidi telling me about the hundreds of letters she received from friends who wrote about the "meaning" of her child's death. "Part of me was enraged," she had said. "How dare anybody presume to tell me there was any good reason for his death?" Heidi was speaking from her position as an initiate. Her friends' efforts to explain what they could not know gave her no comfort.

Initiation requires witnesses to attest to it. You can't just say, "I'm an initiate." There are initiations into some societies that are seen only by other initiates, like those of the Freemasons and many other fraternal organizations, but the more public the initiation, the wider the area of acknowledgment for it within the society, the more profound the effect on society at large and the more profoundly effective the initiate may be afterward.

At Sergio's initiation the entire community was present, including children of all ages. By bearing witness, the community and others in attendance, like myself, got a glimpse, a shivery idea of what an initiate goes through—enough to make us understand the courage it requires, enough to instill enormous respect among us.

When a child dies, there are also witnesses to the survivors' ordeal. We are both drawn to and horrified by the death of other people's children, in part because we are so terrified of the possibility of the death of our own children. Winnie's funeral for Seth and Jill comes to mind, with television coverage and strangers weeping in the packed church, all witnesses to two families' anguished initiation.

From the beginning, as witnesses, we lavish our attention on the child's family. We write and phone; the child's classmates send letters. A notice of the death appears in the local paper and attracts even more witnesses. Then we watch for a long, long time to see how the family is holding up. As witnesses, we wonder if we could do as well.

Initiation includes chaos: the din, the ringing in our ears, the dizziness, the lightheadedness, the nausea, the wild distortion, the confusion, the horror. Initiation is an awful assault on the senses for all those touched by the death of a child in the family. For some time after her son Zach's death, Barbara told me she remained disoriented and in a state of shock. During the first year afterward, she came to rely on barbiturates to relieve her night anxieties. These were symptoms of the chaos she was living. By the time I met her, she had gotten through that aspect of what we might call her initiation and had given up using sleeping pills except very rarely. But many individuals do develop substance-abuse problems in an effort to ease the chaos they feel after the death of a child.

Initiation requires courage. Fearlessness is not demanded of the initiate, but bravery, endurance, and fierce determination to get through it are required. Think of the courage it takes to hear of the death of our child, to wake up every morning to the shock of it all over again, to get out of bed to an agony of pain, to accept the overwhelming, often smothering attention of well-meaning friends when all we really want is to be left alone, to face the idea of a future without our child or the crushed and sorry faces of our colleagues when we return to work.

It took remarkable courage for Winnie to come to therapy. It took courage for Barbara to abandon the deceptive comfort of her sleeping pills. Evelyn discovered her courage in the course of her initiation, and it allowed her to separate from Daniel with a kind of grace that I have not seen before or since.

The most dramatic and the most hideous part of an initiation is its *blood sacrifice*. The blood is the initiate's own blood, or it is a symbol of the initiate's blood. Sometimes the initiate is cut and his blood sprinkled on the earth. Sometimes the initiate is drenched in the blood of an animal, as Sergio was.

In the case of initiation by the death of our child, the blood sacrifice is neither metaphorical nor symbolic. It's not necessary that our children's blood be literally spilled in a violent accident, as Zach's and Sara's was, or in a murder, as Seth's and Jill's was or because of surgery or a transfusion, as Jesse's was. When our children die, *they* are our blood sacrifice. It is *our* blood that flowed through their veins.

Initiation requires a period of isolation. Physically, psychically, emotionally, intellectually, we need time to adjust to our new circumstances after the death of our child. We need time to accustom ourselves to our new selves, empty of those parts of us that have died, that have been shocked and shaken out of us in the process of the initiation. Rebuilding ourselves as someone new may take place over a short period, as in Sergio's ritual isolation, or over many years, as is more likely when a child dies.

In other cultures the period of isolation is *crucial* and respected by the initiate and the community. In Western cultures we often struggle against the natural desire to be alone, to disconnect the phone, to not answer the door. We have the notion that we should be getting on with life as it used to be, not realizing yet that life will never be the same again. "When does this grieving end?" is a frequently asked question after a child dies. We want to rush through it; we're desperate for it to be over.

And it is common for those who want to "help" the family who has lost a child to perpetuate the myth that "getting over" or beyond or past one's grief is the way to go, and the faster the better. In fact, people don't "get over" the death of their child. But they can hope to get better, and a period of seclusion and separation, which need not be stringent or absolute, seems vital to that process of absorbing what has happened and learning to breathe again.

Isolation and the strong desire for isolation usually occur right after the initiating event, as Sergio was led away right after the blood ritual in his temple. Traditional Jews isolate themselves for seven days immediately after burying a loved one, not leaving their homes, although they will receive visitors. But for the most part we put aside our natural inclination. Our culture asks us to do anything but seek a little solitude. Family and friends fly to our side. We have to make arrangements, to deal with people on the phone and in person. We're counseled to keep busy, to seek company after the natural gathering of friends and family and the natural outpouring of condolences have ceased.

Our culture doesn't recognize the value of some isolation after the death of a child, and this can make our need to be alone feel full of conflict. While I have known some Westerners, like my client Heidi, who used time alone in the early days after her child's death to try to connect with his spirit, to help him adjust, this is rare. Without social acknowledgment and recognition, we usually end up stealing the time we need by ourselves. We don't really know how to use that time for more than sadness, and we feel guilty and ashamed for not feeling any better any sooner.

Initiation requires the death of an aspect of oneself. Anyone who has lost a child knows the truth of this. The chaos foretells it; the spilling of blood represents it; the period of isolation confirms it. So much of us dies with our children.

Our future as we envisioned it is gone. The death of an only child may be the end of the family, as in the end of a bloodline. The death of an only child is the death of ourselves as mother or father, just as the big sister loses that part of her identity when her only younger sibling dies.

The death of the child may also be a death knell for a marriage and with it one's identity as a wife or husband.

The death of our children can become the death of our spiritual self.

The death of our children can be seen as the death of the child that every adult holds in spirit and in mind—the ability to face the day with delight and curiosity, the ability to move carelessly in the world.

And beyond the death of the child is the death of our innocence. We may regain or remake parts of ourselves, but we will not regain this.

But we may become spiritual people again and may be able to laugh again and may become mothers and fathers again. We just won't be the same spiritual people; we may not laugh at the same things as before; and we will be different mothers and fathers than we were before.

Life After Initiation

Because we are not accustomed to looking at a child's death as a means of initiation, we don't talk about it in those terms. Instead we think about life after our child dies as a series of gaping deficits. Over time we may refashion a life, but it will be a life without the physical presence of the child and with so much that we used to be and believe stripped away.

Without the language to liken our child's death to an initiation for the survivors, we may not realize how our sight has changed, how much we used to see in black and white, how a world of grays exists now. We may not become aware for quite a while of how those shades of gray create a depth of vision and perspective that we couldn't see before.

Without a vocabulary to honor the wisdom and revaluing of life that eventually replace lost innocence, we may not realize that we contain anything but despair, even years after the death of our child.

Without the word *initiation,* we might miss what the loss of our child has left in its wake. We will not look for the well of courage that has opened to us. We may not know it's there.

As an initiate, Sergio did know to look for his courage. He expected to have new wisdom in exchange for his innocence, because his culture had taught him that these were the fruits of initiation. He expected to discover a well of power that was unavailable to him before. Along with such powers he knew he would bear great responsibilities. Initiates to the Egun-gun are in service to their communities. They are as likely to be called upon as healers when a child is ill as to assist community rituals and celebrations. In addition, once initiated, the Egun-gun become keepers of their people's long-dead ancestors.

Sergio knew that part of his initiation was access to the ancestors, to the realm of spirits. But we don't look for a similar access when our children die. Even though we may continue a dialogue with our child after death, we do it surreptitiously. Our community does not wholeheartedly support us with acceptance or recognition for this particular access. Our community doesn't have the language we are using here.

But if we applied the word *initiate* to the otherwise nameless condition of having lost a child, and added all of its themes to the language of this loss, how much broader the dialogue would be! And if it is true that initiation gives us access to the realm of spirit, then maybe the word can lift us up after we have been brought so low. And maybe from there it will be possible to be "full," as Sergio came to be.

CHAPTER TWELVE

Life as an Initiate

In talking to her for this book, I asked Heidi, whose son had been swept off the rocks in Maine sixteen years earlier, how she looked at that event now, after so long, and how she believed it had affected her life. This is what she told me:

> I hold it in so many different ways, Sukie. I almost hesitate to say it, but it's been the greatest learning of my entire life. Whatever I had believed in up until Lawrence drowned, it was just wrong. It was wrong when he died; it was wrong how he died; it was painful; it was horrible. You know I was very big on trying to make meaning out of things. But it was a meaningless event. There was nothing right about it, no reason to it, but it changed my life in a very profound way.
>
> It connected me very deeply to something in myself, and it humbled me. In those years—I was in my thirties—I was an incredibly arrogant person, and humility was not anything that I had an experience of. I really got a sense of my place. I realized that life is so much more powerful than anything I ever thought. Lawrence's death changed my world in ways I could never have imagined. It changed my feelings about myself; it changed how I

decided to live my life. I became less future oriented. It was so clear to me that I could be whisked away in five minutes.

Somehow Lawrence's death gave me permission to become the introvert that I was born to be. Prior to that, I had no permission to do that, but grieving—somehow you're allowed to go inside and be quiet and I began to write poetry, which I hadn't done before. It softened me. I had always been such a tough cookie.

I don't mean that I'm weak. I'm not. I'm much stronger than I used to be, but I'm also softer. You know I sit with AIDS patients now? I think Lawrence's death allows me to do that, to be with the grief of people who are dying, to know how to be with their families.

How Are We Different?

When we have gone through the eight stages of initiation, much has changed. We are different inside in the way we think and feel, and different outside, in the world. We have lost our innocence, and we have gained some wisdom about the complex and mysterious workings of the world. While we were powerless in the course of initiation, we walk away from it more powerful people.

We have a new perspective: initiates are often less future oriented, as Heidi observed. Our experience has taught us that neither the past nor the future comes with any guarantees. I think that this new relationship with time is part of what is empowering—because living primarily in the present enables us to focus on what's happening now, what's needed now, which can make us extremely effective people, personally and sometimes even publicly.

Initiates make their way with a kind of interior stillness, an ability to be quiet, to hear what's being said or implied. Maybe the extraordinary sensory assault of initiation has made them this way, so that they seem to see more and hear more than most of us.

Post-initiation, Sergio told me he had found that he could sit with a neighbor in need and impart comfort to that person. His initiation, and his community's respectful appreciation for the man who would emerge from it, seemed to have settled a mantle of authority over his shoulders. He told me he had discovered a knack for giving advice. He had learned how to perform many religious rituals, including those that allow him to assist the community's ancestor spirits, which provide spiritual and practical direction for the Candomblé people.

For Sergio the strengths and gifts that he gained in the course of his initiation came with certain responsibilities and expectations. He knew, and so did his community, that the new wisdom and new abilities that initiation instilled in him both required and enabled him to serve his people. He would apprentice for a certain period before assuming his full position as spiritual counselor, but he already had the veneration of his village.

When we return to the world after the death of our child, we are not received as Sergio was. Our culture is more likely to look at us as victims than as leaders and more likely to pity us than to honor the wiser, more compassionate, more courageous people we can become after the death of our children. But after initiation we have similar strengths and similar gifts to Sergio's. And we, too, have earned them.

These gifts are ours, whether we know it or not, and maybe they always were there inside us. But to be of value to us or to the world, it's necessary to unlock them, to gain access to them. That's what language can do, and that is what, specifically, the word, the concept, the ritual of initiation does. That's what each of its eight stages is meant to do, to break through the emotional barriers, to strip away civilized knowing, to put us in touch with and open the door to certain essential qualities that we could not have touched before or could not have used as well before—qualities of passion, of serenity, of spirit, of insight.

I have met many people who have lost children who do recognize these changes. They use their found or heightened attributes loudly or softly, depending on personal style and inclination. Their contributions to the world are big and small. Some are very visible in their effectiveness. I call these people outer initiates. Some use their gifts in less conspicuous ways. I call these the inner initiates. Both expressions of initiation are of equal value.

How We Make Our Way:
The Outer Initiates

When we finally begin reentry into the world, "healing" is almost a moot issue. Perhaps the healing is finished. Perhaps this is as far as it goes. Perhaps that wounded part of ourselves that needed healing is one of the parts that died in the initiation ritual, or maybe it is one of the remnants that has fallen away in this new atmosphere. Now "living" seems more crucial than "healing," and the critical life question changes from "Why did my child die?" or "When will this grieving end?" to "How shall I make my way?"

Candy Lightner, whose twelve-year-old daughter was killed by a drunk driver, may be the most well-known outer initiate, whose "way" was to launch the crusade we now know as MADD (Mothers Against Drunk Driving). When she emerged from her "devastating enlightenment," as I have heard it called, Candy Lightner discovered that alongside her courage was a great passion and tenacity. She turned these gifts into a force for a better, safer world by helping to educate, prevent, deter, and punish drunk drivers. MADD has influenced judicial reforms —among them, raising the legal drinking age to twenty-one across the country—and it has chapters in all fifty states and internationally.

Interestingly, Candy Lightner receives the kind of deferential respect in our culture that initiates in other cultures are accustomed to. She is sought after. What she says is taken seriously. She is a frequent guest on national television and radio talk shows and appears before Congress to lobby for stricter drunk-driving laws. She has been a recipient of the President's Volunteer Action Award. These are the honors and influence due an initiate, but they are rarely acknowledged as such in our western world, except among the circle of people whose lives they touch.

Candy Lightner's circle has been nearly global. More often the outer initiate radiates within a somewhat smaller community than that, as was the case with Winnie and with Myra and Robert.

Winnie Now

Winnie, whose grandson Seth was murdered, had never been one to listen to her "inner voice." She had little respect for the concept of "intuition," as she explained to me early in our time together, pronouncing the word with some disdain. I don't think she ever really considered looking for answers to personal problems inside. She looked to God. She came to me. She was accustomed to finding solutions on the outside.

Our four "test" sessions turned into ten months of sessions before Winnie thanked me warmly for my time and said good-bye. By then I had become very fond of her, and I know she felt the same toward me. I received Christmas cards from her for a few years, and then I moved to the West Coast and we lost touch.

In 1996 the son who had sent Winnie to me all those years ago phoned to tell me that she had passed away. She was eighty-seven years old. She had died in her sleep while she napped. I was sad to learn of her death and grateful to her son for telling me, and since I was going to be back in New York during the week of her funeral, I decided to take the train up to Boston to say good-bye.

I remembered Winnie's description of the enormous church where her grandson's funeral was held. Hers took place in that same church, so large that the hundreds of people who gathered there to honor her seemed an intimate group. The choir sang "How Great Thou Art." The priest who conducted the service was very young. After the homily he read the names of twelve people who came up to the front of the church to speak about Winnie.

One of these was her oldest daughter, Seth's mother, whom I had never met. I was shocked at how much like Winnie she looked—tall, willowy, beautifully dressed, aristocratic. She was in her early sixties, I thought, ten years younger than Winnie had been when she first came to see me.

For the next hour these dozen people spoke lovingly, respectfully, with tears and with laughter about Winnie as a mother, as a grandmother, as a Christian, and as a master bridge player! And among the family, the members of her church group, and a woman who had been Winnie's friend since they were both sixteen years old was also a member of a group called Parents of Murdered Children,[1] which Winnie had joined not long after our meetings in the early 1980s.

I was astonished to learn that Winnie had become a much-beloved, hard-working, ever-present, unofficial counselor to and spokesperson for families of murdered children. One after another, her colleagues and friends spoke of her "quiet presence," her ability to "listen with her whole heart," her "humility in the face of suffering," along with her "never take no for an answer" approach to whatever she considered necessary for her families.

Winnie had been anything but a quiet presence during our sessions, but what her family and friends described is part of every initiate's potential for sensitivity, her ability to be in the present and to face up to suffering because she's been there, knows the terrain, and knows it can be survived. Winnie took what she had learned about this special form of suffering and offered it to families in need. It is not too much different from what Sergio does when he sits with a neighbor and comforts him.

Myra and Robert Now

The last time I saw them together as clients, Robert and Myra had been so disillusioned in their faith that I wondered how or if they would ever return to God. But when she and I met again all those years later to talk about "seeing" Sara as she would have looked at twenty, Myra assured me that they hadn't given up the struggle to be in a relationship with a spiritual life so easily.

They took some yoga classes together and picked up some books on Tibetan Buddhism; they explored a world of esoteric philosophies. Then they heard about a movement called Jewish Renewal, a faction that has reframed the practice of Judaism to emphasize rediscovering the mystical aspects of the religion. The Jewish Renewal movement asks its members, "How can we access God in our own lives and make life better for the people around us?"[2] It was a question Myra and Robert could find satisfying answers for.

"We were invited to a communal Passover seder," Myra told me. "We were nervous. It had been years since we had observed any of the holidays, but there we met an instant family."

For a couple who had been so insular, they were surprised at how easily they fit into a group of a dozen or so families. "Not that they were a substitute for Sara, by any means," Myra told me, "but they fulfilled the family part that we were missing. And they cared enormously about Sara, about our loss, and about keeping her name. They were really our inspiration for 'the fleet.' "

"The fleet," Myra explained, consisted of two emergency helicopters now installed at an emergency heliport named after Sara in the popular ski resort area where she had spent her last weekend. The entire project had been financed by five nearby resorts, the helicopter manufacturer, and corporate contributions, all of which had been actively recruited by Sara's parents.

"The experience was exhilarating," Myra said. "We'd never been especially outgoing. Well, you remember. We'd never asked anything of anybody. But raising the funds for this was really transformative. It opened us up. Our spirits revived. We discovered we could feel again. Feel very deeply. And accomplish a lot."

Making Our Way: The Inner Initiates

Many people whom we are calling "initiates"—who have been lost and found by this terrible route of having lost a child—do not go *out* to change the world. They may still take up a cause or find a "good work," but these are footnotes to their lives, not causes. Inner initiates are practically never activists.

Still, they come away from initiation with new eyes that make them more perceptive, with new minds that make them more understanding, and with hearts that have broken *open* and can now hold so much more than they ever did before. Heidi is one of these kinds of people, making a difference in the world *by virtue of the kind of person she has become.* These are her words:

Let me tell you something. I had a wonderful friend in London, a brilliant Gestalt therapist. After Lawrence's death she and I talked a lot about children and about loving a child, and after many many conversations she said she could see what a *gift* the loss of a child would be.

Well, I was sick to death at the idea of that, that Lawrence's death was any gift, because it was not yet in my experience.

And now it is true, in the sense of the impact of Lawrence's death on my life and my family's life. I don't mean that it was *meant* as a gift. I don't mean that I'm glad he died. I mean the death of a child touches people and makes something else happen.

I believe my family lives in greater harmony and with greater love and respect than it might have. It's like a saving grace.

Evelyn Now

With or without a cause, initiates can help other people simply by being "fully human" in a world where humanity is so often lacking. I think of Evelyn as someone who is valuable because of the fullness she carries inside her. Evelyn is an inner initiate with a circle of influence as luminous as any outer directed initiate's, but her circle is smaller.

In passing, you might think she is absolutely ordinary. She loves her kids; she has a close group of women friends; she's quietly begun to date. We all know people like Evelyn, who don't appear particularly ambitious in the world, who are smart enough but not "intellectuals," who can think of nothing better than spending four hours at a stretch in their garden by themselves, who are perfectly, happily, self-contained.

Get close to Evelyn, and it becomes quite apparent that she is someone special. She is someone who has found her courage, who has come into her own, who has gotten better after being so badly hurt. Evelyn carries scars, but she is also a whole person now, and in some indefinable way it shows, and when you are with her, you can feel it.

These quiet people, who know the worst, who have been through the chaos, the blood sacrifice, the isolation, and the death of themselves, who may not be outwardly active in the world may still be living fully realized lives, and every person they touch may well walk away with a gift from them.

Postscripts

There are many clients whose stories I cannot conclude in these last pages because we've lost track of one another over the years. A few people stay in touch by sending an occasional note. A year after my last session with Andrea, the attorney whose baby was stillborn, who couldn't stop crying, I received a birth announcement from her. "It's a boy!" it read, and inside she had written, "Nine pounds, eight ounces of pure joy!"

I don't know what became of Barbara and John, whose son, Zach, died as a teenager and whose bedroom had remained untouched for many years. Our therapy sessions had ended without much visible benefits, but I have reason to be optimistic and to think of them as outer initiates. Several years after our last session, I received a postcard from Barbara—mailed from China—with this message: "Dear Sukie, I never knew the world was so wide. John retired last year and is showing me. Love, Barbara."

The note seemed so *expansive* for the Barbara I had known who was still in a kind of isolation, still in the process of her initiation. If her card was any indication, then this Barbara was one who had come through it, who could walk out the door of Zach's room and into an expanded life—as far away as China.

What If It Were True?

As we have done in previous chapters, let's test the idea of initiation against the measure of our imagination and ask, "What if we perceived the entire hideous experience of losing a child, from the event itself, through the long chaotic ordeal afterward, as a kind of unasked-for initiation into a deeper experience and knowledge of the world? What would it mean for the bereaved family of the child who died, and what for those of us who wish we could offer some comfort to that family?

If we accept the loss of our children as a kind of initiation, then we no longer have to rise above our pain or get over it or even around it. As initiates, we go through it—we incorporate our pain. And that pain becomes part of our organism, part of our "fullness," and like everything else on the other side of initiation, it is different from the raw, tempestuous confusion of the past. As initiates returning to life, we can truthfully say, *"This pain is part of my strength. This pain is part of my knowledge."*

If those of us who have lost a child were understood to be initiates, then it would not be necessary for us to put our children behind us, as we are often encouraged to do. Instead we could *include* our children in our lives and they could become part of our organism, part of our "fullness." For some people these children might become a dynamic driving force, as Candy Lightner's little girl did. For some, they might become a force for personal strength and inner connectedness, as Lawrence turned out to be for Heidi.

If we saw ourselves and others saw us as initiates, and if we understood that what was happening to us, horrible as it might be, was an initiation, two things could result. We might finally have a context, a language, for what was previously unfathomable and without which we have been wrenched away from our children, ourselves, and our greater communities.

And if we saw ourselves and others saw us as initiates, we could move from being just victims to being people able to draw on our own resources of courage, of vision, and of life. And then we might see ourselves as full human beings, and others would recognize us too.

It doesn't happen overnight. The process of initiation itself may seem to take forever. And returning can take many years. But we can come back, and when we do, I suspect it is with the blessings of our departed children.

Self-Help Resources

The following organizations may be helpful to those coping with the loss of a child:

American Association of Suicidology (AAS)
2459 South Ash Street
Denver, CO 80222
(303) 692-0985
Leads families of suicide victims to local resources such as survivors' groups, literature about suicide, and other help for the bereaved.

Bereaved Parents USA
P.O. Box 95
Park Forest, IL 60466
(708) 748-7672
Provides a network of peer support groups, newsletter, resources, and special help.

The Candlelighters Childhood Cancer Foundation
1901 Pennsylvania Ave. NW, Suite 101
Washington, DC 20006
(202) 659-5136
Supports parents of children who have or who have had cancer, from the beginning of diagnosis, throughout treatment, and on to either cure or death. Membership includes a free bimonthly newsletter.

Centering Corporation
 1531 N. Saddle Creek Road
 Omaha, NE 68104-5064
Maintains a list of resources and books on child loss, grief, and bereavement.

The Compassionate Friends (TCF)
 P.O. Box 3696
 Oak Brook, IL 60522-3696
 (708) 990-0010
A national and international organization and one of the most prominent and respected self-help volunteer groups for bereaved parents, grandparents, and siblings. Offers programs, resources, telephone support, and a library. Most TCF groups meet monthly. There are 655 chapters in the United States alone. TCF publishes a quarterly national newsletter, a quarterly sibling newsletter and books to order, and holds annual national and regional conferences.

The Doughy Center
 The National Center for Grieving Children and Families
 P.O. Box 86852
 Portland, OR 97286
 fax: (503) 777-3097, e-mail: www.doughy.org

Helping Other Parents in Normal Grieving (HOPING)
 Sparrow Hospital
 P.O. Box 30480
 Lansing, MI 48909-7980
 (517) 483-3873
 Information and resources for bereaved parents.

Hope for the Bereaved, Inc.
 4500 Onondaga Street
 Syracuse, NY 13219
 (315) 475-4673
Carries books and resources on bereavement for adults and children, including information on how to form support groups.

Grief Recovery Help Line
(800) 445-4808
A public service of the Grief Recovery Institute Foundation, free of charge, providing personal help with loss and grief.

M.I.S.S. (Mothers in Sympathy and Support)
Coordinator, Joanne Caciatore (602) 979-1000
A grass-roots organization supporting parents one-on-one after the death of an infant or young child. Grief workshops available for professionals to work with families during and after the death of their child.

Mothers Against Drunk Driving (MADD)
Attn: Inquiries Dept.
669 Airport Frwy., Suite 310
Hurst, TX 76053
Dedicated to educating the public about the dangers of drunk driving, MADD works for stronger laws against drivers who drink. MADD publishes a quarterly newsletter.

National SIDS Clearinghouse
8201 Greensboro Dr., Suite 600
McLean, VA 22102
(703) 821-8955
Provides helpful literature on sudden infant death syndrome (SIDS), including reports on the latest medical research.

Parents of Murdered Children (POMC)
1739 Bella Vista
Cincinnati, OH 45237
(513) 242-8025
Offers local support groups for parents and families and helps families who have unresolved legal issues. Sponsors a traveling "Murder Wall," which carries tributes to murdered loved ones, and "Parole Block," which helps keep murderers in prison. Chapters exist throughout the United States.

Pen-Grandparents
P.O. Box 3304
Jasper, AL 35502
(205) 384-3053
A correspondence network for bereaved grandparents.

A Place to Remember
deRuyter Nelson Publications, Inc.
1885 University Avenue, Suite 110
St. Paul, MN 55104
Offers special resources on infant death, books, and special remembrances to help parents and family members.

Pregnancy and Infant Loss Center
1415 East Wayzata Blvd.
Wayzata, MN 55391
(612) 473-9372
Provides information and counseling services.

Resolve Through Sharing
La Crosse–Lutheran Hospital
1910 South Ave.
La Crosse, WI 54601
(608) 785-0530, ext. 3675
Provides information for professionals and families who have lost babies through miscarriage, stillbirth, or newborn death.

The Samaritans Safe Place
33 Chestnut St.
Providence, RI 02903
(401) 272-4044
Self-help support for survivors of suicide victims.

SHARE (Source of Help in Airing and Resolving Experiences)
   St. Joseph's Health Center
   300 First Capitol Drive,
   St. Charles, MO 63301-2893
   (800) 821-6819; fax: (314) 947-7486
Support in dealing with the loss of a newborn, stillbirth, miscarriage, or ectopic pregnancy. Bimonthly newsletter, network of worldwide support groups, literature, referrals.

About the Senior Researchers for the Institute for the Study of the Afterdeath

The Institute for the Study of the Afterdeath engages many people throughout the world to gather its data. These colleagues, called senior researchers, live within the country and are familiar with the particular group or groups we investigated. Frequently the researchers themselves have suggested tribes or cults that are rich in after-death beliefs.

All senior researchers have full access to the groups upon whom they report, and all are trusted and welcomed by the elders of the people. Some have been born into the group and left to receive more formal education. Others are academics who have devoted their life careers to studying the groups we were interested in. One is a therapist utilizing her group's traditional teachings in contemporary healing. One is an anthropologist-cartographer; two are emeritus professors; another is a maskmaker-priest; and the remaining senior researchers are professors of the humanities.

The following is a list of the senior researchers associated with the institute and the people whose views they have shared with us.

Senior Researchers in Africa

In association with the Yoruba people:
Bade Ajuwon, Ph.D., Director
Institute of Cultural Studies
Obafemi Awolowo University
Ile-Ife, Nigeria

The Yoruba are an important West African ethnic people residing mainly in the southwestern part of Nigeria but also in the Republic of Benin and Togo. The Yoruba culture has a strong influence among the Creole population of Sierra Leone and in the African Diaspora, especially in Brazil, Trinidad, and Tobago, and in Cuba, where the Yoruba language has been preserved as a ritual language.

The Yoruba pantheon of gods is said to be about four hundred in number, and each of the gods has a specific duty to perform on earth in relation to human beings. The Yoruba world view deals extensively with opposition issues of birth and death, heaven and earth, night and day, success and failure.

In association with the Yoruba community elders of Nigeria:
Samuel Osunwole, Ph.D.
Institute of African Studies
University of Ibadan
Ibadan, Nigeria

In Nigerian culture elders are those fifty-five years and older who possess necessary leadership qualities, wisdom, and experience about community life and traditions. They are dependable resources for cultural information, which they pass on to their children from generation to generation through informal education such as talks, songs, stories, and poems. From such oral transmissions, a people's myths, history, and tradition become a living reality. Most elders in their seventies and older claim that they see beyond this earth and can contact and communicate with the ancestor spirits in heaven.

In association with the babalawo:
O. O. Adekola
Institute of African Studies
University of Ibadan
Ibadan, Nigeria

The history, philosophy, religion, policy, economy, language, and all other Yoruba cultural customs or institutions are embedded in the Ifa literary corpus and are believed by traditional Yoruba men and women to be an embodiment of the Yoruba culture. The *babalawo* (Ifa priests) are trained experts in the Ifa divinations, and their profession is hereditary. They are highly respected and feared by their people, who believe that these priests possess esoteric powers.

In association with the Igbo healers, diviners, and experts:
   Ernest N. Emenyonu, Ph.D.
   Visiting Professor
   African and Afro-American Studies Department
   Brandeis University
   Waltham, Massachusetts
   Formerly Provost and Chief Executive
   Alvan Ikoku College of Education
   Owerri, Imo State, Nigeria

The Igbo, who number over 15 million people, are one of the three major ethnic groups in Nigeria (the Hausa and the Yoruba are the others), which together make up 65 percent of Nigeria's population of 101 million. The Igbo (the name describes the people, the language, and the territory) are known for their migrant, egalitarian, and communal tendencies. Although they live in all parts of Nigeria and West Africa in general, their ancestral homes are in the Nigerian states of Imo, Anambra, Enugu, Abia, Delta, and Eboyi. The traditional Igbo believe in a supreme God and a galaxy of minor deities and ancestors. Today the Igbo continue to maintain a strong sense of family and community as a way of life and at the same time are considered to be among the most refined and educated Nigerians.

In association with the Yakurr people:
   A. U. Iware, Ph.D., Former Acting Director
   Institute of African Studies
   University of Ibadan
   Ibadan, Nigeria

The Yakurr people, estimated to number about half a million, are rain forest dwellers located in the Cross River state of southeastern Nigeria. They are essentially a subsistence-farming community, with yams as their prestige crop. Despite their exposure to the strong winds of modernity from the West in the form of education and exotic social habits, their traditional beliefs and customs have remained remarkably intact, especially in regard to ceremonies concerning death and the burial of children.

In association with the Nembe-Ijo:
　　Professor Emeritus E. J. Alagoa
　　History Department
　　Faculty of the Humanities
　　University of Port Harcourt
　　Port Harcourt, Nigeria

The Nembe are one of the eastern subgroups of the Ijo ethnic group spread across the delta of the Niger River along the eastern coastal region of Nigeria. They have occupied this unique ecological niche for over eight thousand years, and their culture, worldview, and political economy are reflective of their environment.

Reports on the Nembe for the Institute for the Study of the Afterdeath are based on Professor Alagoa's personal knowledge. Having been born and raised in the region, he has also devoted thirty-plus years to academic research into the history and culture of the group. Reports draw also from recent interviews with a seventy-three-year-old female of the community and a fifty-nine-year-old male member of the community, fourteen of whose thirty children have died.

Senior Researcher in India

In association with the Mahapatras, Ojha shamans, and Baha'is:
　　Vimal Mehra, Sociologist
　　Varanasi, India

The Mahapatras are a group of outcast Brahmans who perform certain death rituals for a bereaved family. Serving as "carriers" of things needed by the soul in the afterlife, for a fee the Mahapatra is said to "carry the shadow of death." "Consignments" are made by donating requisite goods to a Mahapatra in the name of the dead or feeding the Mahapatra food that is meant for the spirit. The Mahapatras are invariably male and take over from the moment the body reaches the funeral site. They do not come to the dead person's house because this is considered inauspicious for the living people in the household.

The Ojha shamans are a class of healers in India who are routinely consulted when any member of a family is suspected of being possessed by an evil spirit. The Ojhas not only act as exorcists but are able to secure peace for a spirit that has not found peace after death. In other words, if the rituals performed by a Mahapatra are not effective, the Ojha completes the job. Even if he fails to find peace for the spirit, the Ojha can at least "nail down" the spirit with certain rituals to prevent it from harming living people.

The Baha'i religion was founded in the nineteenth century in Iran by the prophet Bahaullah, who was then repeatedly banished and persecuted as a heretic by the ruling Muslim orthodoxy. Even today the Baha'is are severely persecuted in their home country. The Bahais seek to uncover the underlying spiritual unity of all religions and believe that various prophets and incarnations revered by different faiths all derive from a common source. For instance, they believe that all divine beings (Jesus, Mohammed, Krishna, Buddha, and others) were incarnations of the same God and that fundamentally all religions are one.

People of every creed and race, across all five continents, are followers of the Baha'i faith. The Baha'i permanent headquarters, the Global Justice Temple, is in Haifa, Israel.

Senior Researcher in Brazil

Under the general direction of:
  Edmundo Barbosa
  Initiativa Gaia
  São Paulo, Brazil

In association with the Spiritists:
  John M. Zerio, Ph.D.
  President of the Allan Kardec Educational Society
  Philadelphia, PA

The Spiritist doctrine represents a life vision predicated on the existence and survival of consciousness, the continuous progress of the spirit, reincarnation, the acceptance of human sensitivity to paranormal events, and an unconditional commitment to living according to the ethical teachings of the Christian gospel. The doctrine inspires a way of life centered on personal responsibility, active service to one's fellow human beings, and continuous effort at self-transformation and social improvement. It does not have any of the attributes of formal religions, but it strongly promotes the connection with God through prayer and meditation. The doctrine was compiled and formulated by Allan Kardec, a French philosopher and scientist, in the mid-1800s. Christian Spiritists and their centers are found in Europe, Latin America, the United States, and Canada.

In association with the Candomblé and the Egun communities:
Ade Rodrigue Grassa, therapist
Bahia, Brazil

Candomblé is an Afro-Brazilian religion that includes religious elements from Roman Catholicism and the African Fon and Yoruba cultures (historically linked to Brazil by the slave trade). Candomblé ritual includes rhythmic drumming and dances that induce trance states, as well as possession by spirits. The rituals invoke deities from the Afro-Brazilian pantheon, which incorporate in initiates to socialize, counsel, and provide spiritual support to the faithful.

The cult of the Egun is an aspect of Candomblé dedicated specifically to the dead and the world after death where the spirits of the Candomblé ancestors, known as Egun, the living dead, reside. The Egun cult is a male initiatic cult whose basic function is to invoke the spirits of the ancestors, who return to this life to dance during public ceremonies and serve as counselors to their religious community.

And in general:
Dr. Hernando Guimaraes Andrade
São Paulo, Brazil

Senior Researcher in Indonesia

In association with the Balinese and the Toraja:
   Max Karlheinz Knaus-Rojas, Anthropologist
   Sulawesi, Indonesia

The Balinese are an ethnic group of around 3.5 million people living on the small tropical island of Bali, one of the more than 16,000 islands in the Indonesian archipelago. Their culture and belief system strongly relate to Hinduism, which found its way from ancient India to Sumatra and Java and retreated to the small island of Bali between the fourteenth and sixteenth centuries. Within Indonesia the Balinese culture and religion represent a minority group. Most of the country is influenced by Islam. The Balinese form of Hinduism is strongly related to a former animistic belief system and the more traditional Indian system and is called Agama Hindu Bali, or the Hindu Bali religion.

Balinese are immersed in a strongly structured system of ceremonies and temple festivals connected to the well-being of the gods, the community, and one's personal life.

The name *Toraja* is a collective word for different groups of people living in the highlands of Tana Toraja (Toraja Land) in Sulawesi, Indonesia. Isolated in different mountain valleys, the various groups developed slightly different cultural expressions, architecture, language, after-death beliefs, and rituals.

With about 370,000 people, the Sa'dan Toraja are the largest Toraja group, living in and around the town of Rantepao. Extended families live communally around one clan house, which is the religious and social center for the family. Families that can trace their roots to one common ancestor are connected in one traditional law community that celebrates festivals and ceremonies together. Today every part of life is influenced by the modern Indonesian state, as well as Christian beliefs, but many old beliefs still exist and are practiced.

and
   Judy Slattum and I Made Surya
   Santa Cruz, California, and Bali, Indonesia

APPENDIX C

About the Institute for the Study of the Afterdeath

The Institute for the Study of the Afterdeath is dedicated to researching and documenting after-death beliefs and rituals throughout the world. Its aim is to educate the general public, as well as the health care and legal professions. The Institute takes no position on whether or not an afterdeath actually exists but rather develops cross-disciplinary studies and other activities to encourage and enrich public dialogue on the subject. Its principal current research activity is the first systematic assembling and analysis of data on the afterdeath, by means of its Research Grids and BORIAL.

The Research Grids are a 180-item questionnaire administered by nineteen senior researchers on four continents, including West Africa, India, Brazil, and Indonesia, to representatives of religions, established cults, and other groups. Grid results were analyzed with the particular aim of seeking cross-cultural relationships.

BORIAL (the Brendan O'Reagan Images of the Afterdeath Library) is a computerized archive of images depicting the afterdeath and indexed by country, religion, symbolic features, artists, and major colors.

The ever-accumulating information in these databases lends itself to many forms of presentation, including elementary school curricula, the health profession's curriculum, art books, reference guides, films, and discursive books and articles. An Inventory of Afterdeath Beliefs—a paper-and-pencil packet with a background booklet and eight individual self-assessment booklets—is available for use by caregivers in such settings as hospices and nursing homes, for courses on death and dying and grief counseling, and for the general public.

The Research Grids were published and their results analyzed in the October 1992 and October 1995 issues of OMNI magazine. An overview of Institute findings to date is the subject of *After Death: How People Around the World Map the Journey After Life* (Simon & Schuster), written by the Institute director and founder, Sukie Miller, Ph.D., with Suzanne Lipsett.

The Institute for the Study of the Afterdeath is a nonprofit corporation, and its financial support is provided by private donations and foundation grants. Information about contributing to the Institute's work is available by writing to 1390 N. McDowell Blvd., Suite G, Petaluma, CA 94954. The Inventory of Afterdeath Beliefs can be ordered from the same address for $11.00 each, plus shipping costs. A 20 percent discount is given for orders of twenty or more.

ENDNOTES

Chapter One

1. The Compassionate Friends, in a fund-raising letter signed by Diana Cunningham, Executive Director, 1997.

Chapter Two

1. In the original story, related by Simcha Steven Paull, Ph.D., in "Responding to Bruria's Cry," Bruria and the rabbi have two sons, both of whom are found dead by their mother, but Myra and Robert's rabbi told them the story as written here.

2. Stephen Mitchell, *Genesis,* p. xlii. Although this version of the binding of Isaac is not the one my Sunday School teacher read us, I think Mitchell's language is beautiful here.

3. Kierkegaard wrote of the story in *Fear and Trembling,* as did Theodore Reik in *The Temptation.* Also Aharon Agus, *The Binding of Isaac;* Shalom Spiegel, *The Last Trial;* Jo Milgrom, *The Akedah;* E. Wellisch, *Isaac and Oedipus;* and others.

4. Robert Coles, *The Spiritual Life of Children,* p. 274.

Chapter Three

1. Dr. Catherine Sanders, *How to Survive the Loss of a Child.*
2. Nancy C. Dodge, *Thumpy's Story,* p. 14.
3. Elizabeth Cohen, "The Ghost Baby," p. 84.

4. "For behind every individual father there stands the primordial image of the Father, and behind the fleeting personal mother the magical figure of the Magna Mater. These archetypes of the collective psyche, whose power is magnified in immortal works of art and in the fiery tenets of religion, are the dominants that rule the preconscious soul of the child and, when projected upon the human parents, lend them a fascination which often assumes monstrous proportions." From Carl Jung, *The Collected Works,* vol. 17, pp. 45, 46.

Introduction to Part Two

1. The Simontons' work on "active imagination" is described in their book with James L. Creighton, *Getting Well Again.*

Another pioneer in the field is Martin Rossman, M.D., who has published many books on the healing potential in mental imagery, including *Healing Yourself* and, more recently, *Spontaneous Creative Imagery.*

Chapter Six

1. That most Americans believe in an afterlife is reported in George Gallup, "Spiritual Beliefs and the Dying Process," p. 14.

2. David Van Biema, "Does Heaven Exist?," p. 71.

3. Ibid., p. 73.

4. Peter Kreeft, *Everything You Ever Wanted to Know About Heaven,* p. 19.

5. Alfonso Villa Rojas, *The Maya of East Central Quintana Roo,* p. 151B.

6. Ian Stevenson, *Twenty Cases Suggestive of Reincarnation,* pp. 219–220.

7. David Friend Aberle, *The Psychosocial Analysis of a Hopi Life-History,* p. 20.

8. Ian Stevenson, M.D., of the University of Virginia, the world's foremost researcher into claims of reincarnation, has published numerous scholarly books on the subject. His most recent contribution to the field, published in two volumes, *Reincarnation and Biology: A Contribution to the Etiology of Birth-*

marks and Birth Defects, adds these phenomena to the other indications in favor of the theory.

In their reports to me, senior researchers throughout Africa also remarked upon the frequency of instances of physical similarities—birthmarks or scars—on children who were presumed to be reincarnations of previous children.

9. George Gallup, A Gallup News Service Poll, September 1996: Twenty-two percent of 1,000 adults polled in telephone interviews said they were "sure" of reincarnation, "that is, the rebirth of the soul in a new body after death."

10. Ian Stevenson, *Children Who Remember Previous Lives,* pp. 39–54.

11. Carol Bowman, *Children's Past Lives,* p. 141.

Chapter Seven

1. The 20 percent figure for miscarriage is from *Our Stories of Miscarriage,* Rachel Faldet and Karen Fitton eds., p. 48. Elizabeth Cohen also writes, "Between 15 and 25 percent of pregnancies end in miscarriage," in her story "The Ghost Baby," p. 84.

2. These days it is *not* Catholic doctrine that the fetus is without spirit until the age of three months.

3. N. Adriani and Albert C. Kruyt, *The Bare'e-speaking Toradja of Central Celebes,* p. 488.

4. *Gambe-*jar reference is from Herbert Aschwander, *Symbols of Death,* p. 249.

5. Elizabeth G. Harrison, "Women's Responses to Child Loss in Japan," p. 69.

The "naming" ceremony to establish an identity for the child as a survivor is a custom that crosses cultures. The Nigerian woman in Chapter 6 (page 93) who claimed to have been an *abiku* in previous lives, spoke of the tradition of choosing to die on the Yoruba "eighth-day naming ceremony" as an especially cruel prank. "Unless a baby is named within seven to nine days of its birth . . . it will not outlive its parent of the same sex," Diana Baird N'Diaye repeats in "Yoruba Naming Ceremony."

Even in the United States, when child mortality was at its peak during the early decades of the nineteenth century, in order to mislead the angel of death many children were given aliases until they reached the relative safety of two years (Philippe Aries, *The Hour of Our Death*, p. 232).

6. Samuel Coleman, *Family Planning in Japanese Society*, p. 60.

7. Dennis Klass and Amy Olwen Heath, "Grief and Abortion," p. 1.

8. "Stranded on the riverbank" is from a *New York Times* article by Sheryl WuDunn, "In Japan, a Ritual of Mourning for Abortions," p. A5.

9. The devotional practices following abortion began around the time of the Tokugawa Era (1630–1868), according to Samuel Coleman's *Family Planning in Japanese Society*, p. 60. The number of legal abortions a year in Japan is from Sheryl WuDunn's "In Japan, a Ritual of Mourning for Abortions," p. A5.

10. Elizabeth G. Harrison writes in "Women's Responses to Child Loss in Japan" (pp. 67, 68): "By the mid-1980s the word [*mizuko*] had been broadened to refer to any child who died 'out of order.' "

11. About regret: Dennis Klass and Amy Olwen Heath, "Grief and Abortion," p. 7.

Chapter Eight

1. A national and international organization, with 655 chapters in the United States alone, The Compassionate Friends is one of the most prominent and respected self-help volunteer groups for bereaved parents, grandparents, and siblings. The organization offers programs, self-help groups, resources, telephone support, and a library. (See Appendix A, "Self-Help Resources.")

2. Traditional folk story.

Chapter Ten

1. R. J. Knapp, *Beyond Endurance*, p. 56.

2. David R. Blumenthal, *Facing the Abusing God*, p. 245.

3. Mircea Eliade, *Rites and Symbols of Initiation,* p. x.
4. Ibid., p. 3.

Chapter Eleven

1. I've written about the Return of the Dead ritual in *After Death,* pp. 38–43.
2. Edmundo Barbosa, "The Presence of the Gods," pp. 44, 45.
3. Mircea Eliade, "From a certain [structural] point of view initiations are much alike" is from *The Encyclopedia of Religion,* vol. 7 (Macmillan Publishing Co., 1987), p. 225, and Eliade's *Rites and Symbols of Initiation,* p. 2. The eight major themes of initiation that we discuss here are synthesized from a broad reading of Eliade's work on initiation, most specifically as laid out in *Rites and Symbols.*

Chapter Twelve

1. Founded in 1978, Parents of Murdered Children (POMC) has 38,000 members with 98 chapters in 45 states. It offers support for survivors, contact with other similarly bereaved people, self-help groups, and information. (See Appendix A, "Self-Help Resources.")
2. Simcha Paull Raphael, *Jewish Views on the Afterlife,* pp. 31–34.

BIBLIOGRAPHY

There is a vast literature consisting of books, pamphlets, articles, and published papers on the phenomenon of child death. I found much that was helpful to me in preparing this book, that provided background material for cultures I knew little about, that helped me understand beliefs and practices contrary to those I was taught in my own culture, and that explicated our American way, including both the medical and psychological approaches we take to child loss.

Abade, Maurice. *The Races of Upper Tonkin from Phong-Tho to Lang-Son.* Paris: Société d'Editions Geographiques, Maritimes et Coloniales, 1924.

Aberle, David Friend. *The Psychological Analysis of a Hopi Life-History.* Comparative Psychology Monographs. Berkeley and Los Angeles: University of California Press, 1951.

Adriani, N., and Albert C. Kruyt. *The Bare'e-speaking Toradja of Central Celebes, The East Toradjal.* Vol. 1. Trans. by Jenni Karding Moulton. Amsterdam: Human Relations Area Files, 1968 (original edition, 1950).

Agus, Aharon. *The Binding of Isaac and Messiah: Law, Martyrdom, and Deliverance in Early Rabbinic Religiosity.* Albany, NY: State University of New York Press, 1998.

Allen, Marie, and Shelly Marks. *Miscarriage: Women Sharing from the Heart.* New York: John Wiley and Sons, 1993.

Allende, Isabel. *Paula.* New York: HarperPerennial, 1994.

Andrade, Hernani Guimaraes. *A Case Suggestive of Reincarnation: Jacira &*

Ronaldo. Monograph. São Paulo, Brazil: Brazilian Institute for Psychobio-physical Research, 1980.

Angell, James W. *O Susan! Looking Forward with Hope After the Death of a Child.* Pasadena, CA: Hope Publishing House, 1990.

Aries, Philippe. *The Hour of Our Death.* New York: Knopf, 1981.

Arnold, Joan Hagan, and Penelope Bushman Gemma. *A Child Dies: A Portrait of Family Grief.* Philadelphia: Charles Press, 1994.

Aschwander, Herbert. *Symbols of Death.* Zimbabwe: Mambo Press, 1982.

Babcock, Barbara. *Pueblo Mothers and Children: Essays by Elsie Clews Parsons 1915–1924.* Santa Fe, NM: Ancient City Press, 1991.

Bailey, Alice A. *A Treatise on White Magic, or The Way of the Disciple.* New York: Lucis Publishing Company, 1969.

Barbosa, Edmundo. "The Presence of the Gods: Afro-Brazilian Trance Rituals." *Shaman's Drum,* no. 17 (1989).

Bhardwal, Surinder M., and Kanti Paul Bimal. "Medical Pluralism and Infant Mortality in a Rural Area of Bangladesh." *Social Science and Medicine,* vol. 23, no. 10 (1986).

Black, Karen. "Sudden, Unexpected Pediatric Death: Caring for the Parents." *Pediatric Nursing,* vol. 17 (Nov.–Dec. 1991).

Blumenthal, David R. *Facing the Abusing God: A Theology of Protest.* Louisville, KY: John Knox Press, 1993.

Bolinder, Gustaf. *Indians on Horseback.* London: Dennis Dobson, 1957.

Booth, Father Leo. *When God Becomes a Drug: Breaking the Chains of Religious Addiction and Abuse.* Los Angeles: Jeremy P. Tarcher/Putnam, 1991.

Bowlby, John. "The Process of Mourning." *International Journal of Psycho-Analysis,* vol. 42, parts 4–5 (1961).

Bowman, Carol. *Children's Past Lives: How Past Life Memories Affect Your Child.* New York: Bantam Books, 1997.

Bramblett, John. *When Good-Bye Is Forever: Learning to Live Again After the Loss of a Child.* New York: Ballantine, 1991.

Buber, Martin. *Tales of the Hassidim, The Early Masters.* New York: Schocken Books, 1948.

Buchholz, Ester Schaler. *The Call of Solitude: Alonetime in a World of Attachment.* New York: Simon & Schuster, 1997.

Buscaglia, Leo. *The Fall of Freddie the Leaf: A Story for All Ages.* New York: Slack, 1982.

Buthman, David. *Thin Ice.* Omaha, NE: Centering Corporation, 1990.

Carroll, John. *Guilt: The Grey Eminence Behind Character, History and Culture.* London: Routledge & Kegan Paul, 1985.

Castle, Sarah E. "The (Re)negotiation of Illness Diagnosis and Responsibility for Child Death in Rural Mali." Populations Studies and Training Center, Brown University. *Medical Anthropology Quarterly,* vol. 8, no. 3 (1994).

Clark, Martha Bittle. *Are You Weeping with Me, God?* Nashville, TN: Broadman Press, 1987.

Clarke, Michael. "Depression in Women After Perinatal Death." *The Lancet,* April 28, 1979.

Clayton, Paula, et al. "A Study of Normal Bereavement." *American Journal of Psychiatry,* vol. 125, no. 2 (Aug. 1968).

Cohen, Elizabeth. "The Ghost Baby," *New York Times Magazine,* May 4, 1997.

Cohen, George J. "Children Dead on Arrival: Predictors of Short-Term Family Follow-up." *American Journal of Emergency Medicine,* vol. 2, no. 4 (July 1984).

Coleman, Samuel. *Family Planning in Japanese Society: Traditional Birth Control in a Modern Urban Culture.* Princeton, NJ: Princeton University Press, 1983.

Coles, Robert. *The Spiritual Life of Children.* Boston: Houghton Mifflin, 1990.

Compassionate Friends, The. *Grieving, Healing, Growing.* Hindsdale, IL: Compassionate Friends, 1992.

Cook, Judith A. "A Death in the Family: Parental Bereavement in the First Year." *Suicide and Life-Threatening Behavior,* vol. 13, no. 1 (Spring 1983).

Coppo, P., et al. "Perceived Morbidity and Health Behavior in a Dogon Community." *Social Science and Medicine,* vol. 34, no. 11 (1992).

Coreyell, Deborah Morris. *Good Grief: Healing Through the Shadow of Loss.* Santa Fe, NM: Shiva Foundation, 1997.

David-Neel, Alexandra. *Initiations and Initiates in Tibet.* Berkeley, CA: Shambhala Publications, 1970.

DeFrain, John D., and Linda Ernst. "The Psychological Effects of Sudden Infant Death Syndrome and Surviving Family Members." *Journal of Family Practice,* vol. 6, no. 5 (1978).

Demi, Alice S., and Margaret S. Miles. "Patterns of Normal Grief: A Delphi Study." *Death Studies,* vol. 11, pp. 397–412. Hemisphere Publishing Co., 1987.

Devers, Edie. *Goodbye Again.* Kansas City: Andrews and McMeel, 1997.

Dodge, Nancy C. *Thumpy's Story: A Story of Love and Grief Shared by Thumpy the Bunny.* St. Charles, MO: SHARE, 1984.

Doka, Kenneth J., ed. *Children Mourning, Mourning Children.* Washington, DC: Hospice Foundation of America, 1995.

Dreifuss, Gustav, and Judith Riemer. *Abraham: The Man and the Symbol.* Wilmette, IL: Chiron Publications, 1995.

Dubin, William R., and Jeffrey R. Sarnoff. "Sudden Unexpected Death: Intervention with the Survivors." *Annals of Emergency Medicine,* Jan. 1986.

Eisenbruch, Maurice. "Cross-Cultural Aspects of Bereavement I: A Conceptual Framework for Comparative Analysis." *Culture, Medicine and Psychiatry,* vol. 8 (1984).

———. "Cross-Cultural Aspects of Bereavement II: Ethnic and Cultural Variations in the Development of Bereavement Practices." *Culture, Medicine and Psychiatry,* vol. 8 (1984).

Eliade, Mircea. *Birth and Rebirth: The Religious Meanings of Initiations in Human Culture.* New York: Harper and Brothers, 1958.

———. *Images and Symbols: Studies in Religious Symbolism.* Kansas City: Sheed Andrews and McMeel, 1952.

———. *Rites and Symbols of Initiation: The Mysteries of Birth and Rebirth.* New York: Harper Torch Books, 1958.

Evans, Richard Paul. *The Christmas Box.* New York: Simon & Schuster, 1995.

———. *The Letter.* New York: Simon & Schuster, 1997.

———. *The Time Piece.* New York: Simon & Schuster, 1996.

Faldet, Rachel, and Karen Fitton, eds. *Our Stories of Miscarriage: Healing with Words.* Minneapolis: Fairview Press, 1997.

Faschingbauer, Thomas R., et al. "Development of the Texas Inventory of Grief." *American Journal of Psychiatry,* vol. 134, no. 6 (June 1977).

Folta, Jeannette R., and Edith S. Deck. "The Impact of Children's Death on Shona Mothers and Families." *Journal of Comparative Family Studies,* vol. 19, no. 3 (Autumn 1988).

Frankl, Viktor E. *Man's Search for Ultimate Meaning.* New York: Plenum Press, 1997.

Gallup, George. "Spiritual Beliefs and the Dying Process: A Report on a National Survey Conducted for the Nathan Cummings Foundation." Princeton, NJ: George H. Gallup International Institute, 1998.

Gellman, Marc. "Abraham and Isaac." *Moment,* May–June 1976.

Goldman, Irving. *The Cubeo: Indians of the Northwest Amazon.* Urbana: University of Illinois Press, 1963.

Greene, Liz. *The Astrology of Fate.* York Beach, ME: Samuel Weiser, 1984.

Gunther, John. *Death Be Not Proud: A Memoir.* London: Hamish Hamilton, 1949.

Hagin, Rose A., and Carol G. Corwin. "Bereaved Children." *Journal of Clinical Child Psychology,* Summer 1974.

Harrison, Elizabeth G. "Women's Responses to Child Loss in Japan: The Case of Mizuko Kuyo." *Journal of Feminist Studies in Religion, Special Issue, Rhetorics, Rituals and Conflicts Over Women's Reproductive Power,* vol. 2 (Fall 1995).

Head, Joseph, and S. L. Cranston, eds. *Reincarnation: The Phoenix Fire Mystery.* New York: Julian Press/Crown Publishers, 1978.

Heiney, Sue P. "Sibling Grief: A Case Report." Archives of *Psychiatric Nursing,* vol. 5, no. 3 (June 1991).

Hewitt, J.N.B. "The Iroquoian Concept of the Soul." *Journal of American Folk-Lore,* vol. 8 (1895).

Hill, Mary V. *Angel Children: Those Who Die Before Accountability.* Bountiful, OH: Horizon Publishers, 1973.

Hope, Murray. *The Psychology of Ritual.* Longmead, Shaftesbury, Dorset, UK: Element Books Ltd., 1988.

Jackson, Edgar N. *When Someone Dies.* Philadelphia: Fortress Press, 1971.

Jacobs, Selby, and Adrian Ostfeld. "An Epidemiological Review of the Mortality of Bereavement." *Psychosomatic Medicine,* vol. 39, no. 5 (Sept.–Oct. 1977).

James, E. O. *Origins of Sacrifice: A Study in Comparative Religion.* London: John Murray, 1933.

James, William. *The Will to Believe and Other Essays in Popular Philosophy/ Human Immortality.* New York: Dover Publications, 1956.

Jensen, Amy Hillyard. *Healing Grief.* Redmond, WI: Medic Publications, 1995.

Johnson, Sherry E. *After a Child Dies: Counseling Bereaved Families.* New York: Springer Publishing, 1987.

Jung, Carl. *The Collected Works of C. G. Jung.* Vols. 5 and 17. Princeton, NJ: Princeton University Press, 1954.

———. *Memories, Dreams and Reflections.* New York: Vintage Books, 1989.

Karsten, Rafael. *Indian Tribes of the Argentine and Bolivian Chaco: Ethnological Studies.* Finland: Helsingfors, 1932.

Keyser, Marty. "At Home with Death: A Natural Child-Death." *The Journal of Pediatrics,* vol. 90, no. 3 (1977).

Kierkegaard, Søren. *Fear and Trembling.* Princeton, NJ: Princeton University Press, 1983.

Klass, Dennis. "The Inner Representation of the Dead Child and the World Views of Bereaved Parents." *Omega,* vol. 26, no. 4 (1992–93).

———. *Parental Grief: Solace and Resolution.* New York: Springer Publishing, 1988.

———. "Solace and Immortality: Bereaved Parents' Continuing Bond with Their Children." *Death Studies,* vol. 17 (1993).

———, and Amy Olwen Heath. "Grief and Abortion: Mizuko Kuyo, The Japanese Ritual Solution." *Omega,* vol. 34, no. 1 (1996–97).

Klerman, Gerald L., and Judith E. Izen. "The Effects of Bereavement and Grief on Physical Health and General Well Being." *Advances in Psychosomatic Medicine,* vol. 9 (1977).

Klunger-Bell, Kim. *Unspeakable Losses.* New York: W.W. Norton, 1998.

Knapp, John. *Beyond Endurance: When a Child Dies.* New York: Schocken Books, 1986.

Kolatch, Alfred J. *The Jewish Book of Why.* Middle Village, NY: Jonathan David Publishers, 1981.

Kovarsky, Roslyn Sandra. "Loneliness and Disturbed Grief: A Compassion of Parents Who Lost a Child to Suicide or Accidental Death." Archives of *Psychiatric Nursing,* vol. 3, no. 2 (April 1989).

Krance, Magda. "When Prenatal Tests Bring Bad News." *American Health,* July–Aug. 1989.

Kreeft, Peter. *Everything You Ever Wanted to Know About Heaven But Never Dreamed of Asking.* San Francisco: Ignatius Press, 1990.

Kripalani, Krishna. *Tagore, A Life.* Published by the author, 1971.

Krupnick, Janice L., and Mardi J. Horowitz. "Stress Response Syndromes." Archives of *General Psychiatry,* vol. 38 (April 1981).

Kübler-Ross, Elisabeth. "The Language of Dying." *Journal of Clinical Child Psychology,* Summer 1974.

———. *Questions and Answers on Death and Dying.* New York: Macmillan Publishing Co., 1974.

Lascari, Andre D. "The Dying Child and the Family." *Journal of Family Practice,* vol. 6, no. 6 (1978).

Leahy, Julia. "A Comparison of Depression in Women Bereaved of a Spouse, Child, or a Parent." *Omega,* vol. 26 (1992–93).

Levine, Stephen. *Healing into Life and Death.* New York: Anchor Books Doubleday, 1987.

Lieberman, Saul. "Some Aspects of After Life in Early Rabbinic Literature." *Harry Austryn Wolfson Jubilee Volume,* vol. 2. Jerusalem: American Academy for Jewish Research, 1965.

Lord, Janice Harris. *No Time for Goodbyes.* Ventura, CA: Pathfinder Publishing, 1987.

Lundin, Tom. "Long-term Outcome of Bereavement." *British Journal of Psychiatry,* 1984.

Ma'Sumian, Farnaz. *Life After Death: A Study of the Afterlife in World Religions.* Oxford, UK: Oneworld, 1995.

Matchett, William Foster. "Repeated Hallucinatory Experiences as a Part of the Mourning Process Among Hopi Indian Women." *Psychiatry,* vol. 35 (May 1972).

Meade, Michael. *Men and the Water of Life: Initiation and the Tempting of Men.* San Francisco: HarperSanFrancisco, 1993.

Mellonie, Bryan, and Robert Ingpen. *Lifetimes: The Beautiful Way to Explain Death to Children.* New York: Bantam Books, 1983.

Merlin, Katharine. *Character and Fate: The Psychology of the Birthchart.* London: Arkana, 1989.

Metraux, Alfred. *Report on the Ethnography of the Mataco Indians of the Argentine Gran Chaco.* Buenos Aires: Human Relations Area Files, 1959.

Middleton, John, ed. *Gods and Rituals: Readings in Religious Beliefs and Practices.* Garden City, NY: Natural History Press, 1967.

Miles, Jack. *God, A Biography.* New York: Vintage Books, 1996.

Miles, Margaret Shandor. "Emotional Symptoms and Physical Health in Bereaved Parents." *Nursing Research,* vol. 34, no. 2 (1984).

———. *The Grief of Parents When a Child Dies.* Oak Brook, IL: Compassionate Friends, 1978.

Milgrom, Jo. *The Akedah: The Binding of Isaac.* Berkeley, CA: Bibale Press, 1988.

Miller, Sukie, with Suzanne Lipsett. *After Death: How People Around the World Map the Journey After Life.* New York: Simon & Schuster, 1997.

Miller, William A. *When Going to Pieces Holds You Together.* Minneapolis, MN: Augsburg Publishing House, 1976.

Mitchell, Stephen. *Genesis: A New Translation of the Classic Biblical Stories.* New York: HarperCollins, 1996.

Munday, John S., with Wohlenhaus-Munday, Frances. *I Wasn't Ready.* Ocean City, MD: Skipjack Press, 1991.

Naylor, Audrey. "Premature Mourning and Failure to Mourn: Their Relationship to Conflict Between Mothers and Intellectually Normal Children." *American Journal of the Orthopsychiatric Associations,* Oct. 1982.

N'Diaye, Diana Baird, with Gilbert Ogunfiditimi and Frederick Ogunfiditimi. "Yoruba Naming Ceremony in Washington, D.C." *Festival of American Folklife.* Washington, DC: Smithsonian Institution, 1997.

Nelson, Benjamin, ed. *Birth and Rebirth.* New York: Harper and Brothers, 1958.

Niles, John DeWitt. "Lamkin: The Motivation of Horror." *Journal of American Folklore,* vol. 90, no. 355 (Jan.–March 1997).

Nouwen, Henri. *Walk with Jesus: Stations of the Cross.* Maryknoll, NY: Orbis Books, 1990.

Oliver, Ronald C., and Mary R. Fallat. "Traumatic Childhood Death: How Well Do Parents Cope?" *Journal of Trauma: Injury, Infection and Critical Care,* 1995.

Parrinder, Geoffrey, ed. *World Religions, From Ancient History to the Present.* New York: Facts on File Publishers, 1983.

Paull, Simcha Steven. "Responding to Bruria's Cry: Bereavement Support in the Jewish Community." *Jewish Funeral Director,* vol. 55, no. 2 (Summer 1987).

Pearlman, Eileen M. "Separation-Individuation, Self-Concept, and Object Relations in Fraternal Twins, Identical Twins, and Singletons." *Journal of Psychology,* vol. 124, no. 6 (1990).

Peek, Philip M., ed. *African Divination Systems.* Bloomington: Indiana University Press, 1991.

Pospisil, Leopold J. *The Nature of Law. Transactions of the New York Academy of Sciences.* Series II, vol. 18, no. 8. The Kapauku file: E-5 (1954–1955) 1958 OJ29 Kapauku. New Haven, CT: Yale University Publications in Anthropology, 1954.

Purucker, G., ed. *The Esoteric Tradition.* Vols. 1 and 2. Pasadena, CA: Theosophical University Press, 1935.

Rando, Therese A., ed. *Parental Loss of a Child.* Champaign, IL: Research Press, 1986.

Raphael, Beverly. *The Anatomy of Bereavement.* Northvale, NJ: Jason Aronson, 1994.

Raphael, Simcha Paull. *Jewish Views of the Afterlife.* Northvale, NJ: Jason Aronson, 1996.

Reik, Theodore. *Mystery and the Mountain.* New York: Harper and Brothers, 1959.

———. *Ritual: Psychoanalytic Studies.* New York: International Universities Press, 1946.

———*The Temptation.* New York: George Braziller, 1988.

Remen, Rachel Naomi. *Kitchen Table Wisdom.* New York: Riverhead Books, 1997.

Rosenthal, Ted. *How Could I Not Be Among You?* New York: George Braziller, 1973.

Rossman, Martin. *Healing Yourself: A Step-By-Step Program for Better Health through Imagery.* Sausalito, CA: Institute for the Advancement of Health, 1987.

————. *Spontaneous Creative Imagery: Problem Solving and Life-Enhancing Skills.* Sausalito, CA: Institute for the Advancement of Health, 1997.

Rothman, Juliet Cassuto. *Saying Goodbye to Daniel: When Death Is the Best Choice.* New York: Continuum Books, 1995.

Rowe, Jane, et al. "Follow-up of Families Who Experience Perinatal Death." *Pediatrics,* vol. 62, no. 5 (August 1978).

Roy, Alec, Nancy L. Segal, and Parco Sarchiapone. "Attempted Suicide Among Living Co-Twins of Twin Suicide Victims." *American Journal of Psychiatry,* vol. 152, no. 7 (July 1995).

Russell, Dan, et al. "The Revised UCLA Loneliness Scale: Concurrent and Discriminant Validity Evidence." *Journal of Personality and Social Psychology,* vol. 39, no. 3 (1980).

————. "Social and Emotional Loneliness: An Examination of Weiss's Typology of Loneliness." *Journal of Personality and Social Psychology,* vol. 46, no. 6 (1984).

Sanders, Catherine M. "A Companion of Adult Bereavement in the Death of a Spouse, Child, and Parent." *Omega,* vol. 10, no. 4 (1979–80).

————. "Effects of Sudden vs Chronic Illness Death on Bereavement Outcome." *Omega,* vol. 13, no. 3 (1982–83).

————. *How to Survive the Loss of a Child: Filling the Emptiness and Rebuilding Your Life.* Rocklin, CA: Prima Publishing, 1992.

Savage, Judith A. *Mourning Unlived Lives: A Psychological Study of Childbearing Loss.* Wilmette, IL: Chiron Publications, 1989.

Schatz, William H. *Healing a Father's Grief.* Redmond, VA: Medic Publishing, 1984.

Schiff, Harriet Sarnoff. *The Bereaved Parent.* New York: Penguin Books, 1997.

————. *Living Through Mourning.* New York: Penguin Books, 1986.

Sheskin, Arlene, and Samuel E. Wallace. "Differing Bereavements: Suicide, Natural and Accidental Death." *Omega,* vol. 7, no. 3 (1976).

Simonds, Wendy, and Barbara Katz Rothman. *Centuries of Solace: Expressions of Maternal Grief in Popular Literature.* Philadelphia: Temple University Press, 1992.

Simonton, O. Carl, Stephanie Matthews-Simonton, and James L. Creighton. *Getting Well Again: A Step-By-Step Self Help Guide to Overcoming Cancer for Patients and Their Families.* New York: Bantam Books, 1978.

Singh, Bruce, and Beverly Raphael. "Post Disaster Morbidity and Bereavement: A Possible Rose for Preventative Psychiatry?" *Journal of Nervous and Mental Diseases,* vol. 169, no. 4 (April 1981).

Soreff, Stephen M. "Sudden Death in the Emergency Department: A Comprehensive Approach for Families, Emergency Medical Technicians, and Emergency Department Staff." *Critical Care Medicine,* vol. 7, no. 7 (1979).

Spiegel, Shalom. *The Last Trial: On the Legends and Lore of the Command to Abraham to Offer Isaac as a Sacrifice: The Akedah.* Woodstock, VT: Jewish Lights Publishing, 1950.

Stahl, Abraham. "Parents' Attitudes Towards the Death of Infants in the Traditional Jewish-Oriented Family." *Journal of Comparative Family Studies,* vol. 22, no. 1 (Spring 1991).

Stevenson, Ian. *Children Who Remember Past Lives: A Question of Reincarnation.* Charlottesville: University Press of Virginia, 1987.

———. *Reincarnation and Biology: A Contribution to the Etiology of Birthmarks and Birth Defects.* Vols. 1 and 2. Westport, CT: Praeger, 1997.

———. *Twenty Cases Suggestive of Reincarnation.* Charlottesville: University Press of Virginia, 1974.

Stevenson, Nancy Comey, and Cary Higley Straffon. *When Your Child Dies: Finding the Meaning in Mourning.* Lakewood, OH: Philomel Press, 1981.

Steward, Omer C. *Culture Element Distributions: XIV Northern Paiute, Anthropological Records.* Berkeley: University of California Press, 1941.

Stone, Anthony Philip. *Hindu Astrology: Myths, Symbols and Realities.* New Delhi, India: Select Book, 1981.

Tatelbaum, Judy. *The Courage to Grieve: Creative Living, Recovery, and Growth Through Grief.* New York: Harper & Row, 1980.

Tengbom, Mildred. *Help For Bereaved Parents.* St. Louis: Concordia, 1981.

Tribe, Laurence H. *Abortion: The Clash of Absolutes.* New York: W.W. Norton, 1990.

Van Biema, David. "Does Heaven Exist?" *Time* magazine, March 24, 1997.

Van Gennep, Arnold. *The Rites of Passage.* Chicago: University of Chicago Press, 1960.

Van Vechten, B. D. *The First Year of Forever: Surviving the Death of Our Son.* Menton, OH: Dwight Publishers, 1982.

Vargas, Luis A., et al. "Exploring the Multidimensional Aspects of Grief Reactions." *American Journal of Psychiatry,* vol. 146, no. 11 (Nov. 1989).

Villa Rojas, Alfonso. *The Maya of East Central Quintana Roo.* Publication 559. Washington, DC: Carnegie Institute of Washington, 1945.

Vincent, William R. "The Gift of Listening." *Western Journal of Medicine,* vol. 160, no. 81 (1994).

Weisman, Avery D. "Coping with Untimely Death." *Psychiatry,* vol. 36 (Nov. 1973).

Wellisch, E. *Isaac and Oedipus: A Study in Biblical Psychology of the Sacrifice of Isaac — The Akedah.* London: Routledge & Kegan Paul, 1954.

Westberg, Granger E. *Good Grief.* Omaha, NE: Centering Corporation, 1962.

Whiting, Beatrice Blyth. *Paiute Sorcery.* New York: Viking Fund Publications in Anthropology, 1950.

Willis, Diane J. "The Families of Terminally Ill Children: Symptomatology and Management." *Journal of Clinical Child Psychology,* Summer 1974.

Wolf, Arthur Paul. "Marriage and Adoption in a Hokkien Village," A Thesis for the Graduate School of Cornell University, Sept. 1964.

Wright, Lawrence. "Double Mystery." *The New Yorker,* Aug. 7, 1995.

Wright, Logan. "An Emotional Support Program for Parents of Dying Children." *Journal of Clinical Child Psychology,* Summer 1974.

WuDunn, Sheryl. "In Japan, a Ritual of Mourning for Abortions," *New York Times,* Jan. 25, 1996.

Zighelboim, Jacob. *From Fear to Awe.* Beverly Hills, CA: Toren Publishers, 1996.

Zisook, Sidney, et al. "Measuring Symptoms of Grief and Bereavement." *American Journal of Psychiatry,* vol. 139, no. 12 (Dec. 1982).

for the unborn, 106-08
West Africa, 115-17
Rossman, Martin, 67

Sacrifice, death of child as, 32-33
Sacrifice of Isaac, The (artwork), 32
Safety, loss of, 44
Sanders, Catherine M., 41
Self-help groups, 45
Self-help literature, 31
Self-help resources (list), 169-73
Shame, guilt of, 41, 43, 47
Siblings
   guilt in, 43-45, 59, 60
   see also Surviving children
Simonton, Carl, 67
Simonton, Stephanie, 67
Singapore, 26, 118-19
"Single-minded births," 90
Soul(s), 78
   of dead children, 90
   of stillborn children, 104
   of unborn, 14, 65, 106
Spirit
   choosing its destiny, 91
   in reincarnation, 89
   unborn, 108
Spirit contact, 75-76
Spirit life, 143-44
Spirit of dead child, 71, 90, 104
   communication with, 123-24
   connecting with, 144, 154
   maintaining, 132-33
   return of, 89
Spiritists, 13, 112, 144
   afterlife in belief of, 85-86, 87-88
   beliefs of, 79-82, 125
   communication with dead, 123
   life plans, 71-72
   reincarnation in belief of, 90
Spirits
   access to, 156
   relationship with, 68

Spiritual cities, 79, 86
Spiritual Life of Children, The (Coles), 36-37
Stevenson, Ian, 97
Stillbirth/stillborn, 20, 100-01, 104, 105, 106, 107
Stillness, interior, 158
Substance-abuse problems, 152
Sulawesi, 67
Surviving children, 58-61
Survivors of child death, 19, 20, 31
Survivorship guilt, 41, 42, 43-44, 45, 47
   in siblings, 59

Therapy, 45
Thumpy's Story of Love and Grief, 44
Time
   as continuum, 89, 137
   new relationship with, 158
   in recovery, 141
   understanding of, 83-84
   see also Freezing in time
Tlingit Indians, 89
Toraja, 104
Twins, 27-28, 39-40, 75, 142
   rituals for, 115-17

Umbanda religion, 13
   ritual for summoning spirits of dead children for visits, 89, 125-29, 145, 148
Unborn (the), 112
   acknowledging, 108-09
   language for, 103-08, 109
   reality of, 100-09
   souls of, 14, 65

Vishnu (god), 115
Visualization, 67

Waiting (stage), 13
West (the), 105, 153
   and concept of destiny, 73

A B O U T   T H E   A U T H O R

One of the first researchers to study the cross-cultural dimensions of the afterlife, Sukie Miller, Ph.D., is a practicing psychotherapist and the founder and director of the Institute for the Study of the After-death. Dr. Miller has served on the board of the Jung Institute of San Francisco and the Board of Medical Quality Assurance of the State of California. In 1972 she founded and directed the pioneering Institute for the Study of Humanistic Medicine. She lives in northern California.